Mancia...

A Canadian Expat's Take on Sicilian Life and Cuisine

Diane Gallagher

Mancia di Sanu

A Canadian Expat's Take on Sicilian Life and Cuisine

Mancia di sanu e vivi di malatu.
"Eat with gusto but drink in moderation."
-Sicilian Proverb

Foreword by Veronica di Grigoli

Diane Gallagher

Island2Island Press

For all of our friends – Sicilian and expat – who have been nothing but generous with their time, their knowledge, and their friendship.

Copyright© 2016 by Diane Gallagher

Island2Island Press
Duncan, Canada

All rights reserved. No part of this publication may be reproduced, stored in a retrieval system, or transmitted in any form or by any means, electronic, mechanical, photocopying, recording or otherwise, without prior permission of the publisher.

The information in this book is true and complete to the best of our knowledge. All recommendations are made without guarantee on the part of the author or Island2Island Press. The author and publisher disclaim any liability in connection with the use of this information. For additional information, please contact Island2Island Press, 6460 Diana Drive, Duncan, BC V9L 5V3.

Edited and proofread by Heather Miller
Cover design by Ihor Tur
Photographs by Diane Gallagher, Nick Cacciato, and Pat Hellman
Clip Art by PeterM at openclipart; downloaded through Wikimedia Commons

Printed and bound in the United States

Library and Archives Canada Cataloguing in Publication

Gallagher, Diane, 1961-, author
    Mancia di sanu : a Canadian expat's take on Sicilian life and cuisine / Diane Gallagher.

Includes bibliographical references and index.
ISBN 978-0-9951839-0-2 (paperback)

   1. Cooking, Italian--Sicilian style. 2. Cooking--Italy--Sicily.
3. Sicily (Italy)--Description and travel. 4. Sicily (Italy)--Social life
and customs. 5. Cookbooks. I. Title.

TX723.2.S55G35 2016   641.59458
C2016-903418-6

Acknowledgments

While the words on these pages are mine, they would not be here without the support and help of a number of people. To my friends in Sicily, particularly Linda Chartier Scala and her husband Bruno; Pat Hellman; Diane Johnstone; Franca Tamborello and her mother, Anna and late father, Guiseppe and her husband Tano Passafiume; Saverio Carubia; the Filocco family – Silvestro, Gina, Enzo, Enza and Silvio; Jacek and Marta Kochan; Marta Roversi and Fabrizio Riggio; Gianfranco and Maria – owners of Tutto Regalo; our neighbours Giuseppe and Antonio Vaiana and their wife and mother Anna Pendina.

To my supportive friends in Canada, particularly Neil Tubb who taught me the value of creativity; my amazing cousin, chef Dana McCauley who taught me that instant mac and cheese is not really food; Bill Thompson who often acted as a culinary guinea pig; and my sister-in-law, Tina Short, who generously shared her mother's recipes and family stories with me.

To the readers of my blog, My Sicilian Home.

To the amazing staff at Agenzia Immobiliare My House who helped us buy our Cianciana home – Carmelo Panepinto, Alfonso (Fofo) Martorana, Pierangela Cimó and especially Joe Guida who translates everything for us.

To my incredibly supportive and patient husband, Nick Cacciato, who is publishing this book and my daughter

Miyuki Hayashi who commiserates with all my complaints.

And finally, to the late Bernadette Landy-Lovatt who was my first expat friend in Cianciana and whom I miss every single day I am here.

To all of you, *grazie mille*. Without all of you, this book would not have been written.

About the author:

Diane Gallagher is a retired teacher-librarian who has thrown herself with great gusto into her next career – that of being a writer. She takes her craft very seriously. She continues to educate in less traditional methods and is a passionate advocate for human rights. Diane and her husband Nick bought their old stone Sicilian house in 2012 and spend part of every year living there. She has an adult daughter and is waiting anxiously for the day someone will call her "Gramma".

Foreword

Diane and I first "met" online through our blogs. Although popular these days, blogging is a strange hobby. Some bloggers post wedding or holiday photos with brief or enigmatic commentaries, really intended only for their friends and family; some design a high concept for their blog which they hope will ultimately lead to advertising revenue and, in occasional flights of fancy, turn into the next Huffington Post; and others, like Diane and myself, offer up their private lives as a source of entertainment for strangers anywhere in the world. You have to have a special kind of character to do this. You have to be excited when a stranger who starts chatting to you online from a country far away mentions they will be in your neck of the woods next week, and would you like to meet for coffee and cake? You have to enjoy looking for the kind of quirks and foibles in the people around you that will probably entertain your fellow man. Above all, you have to be the kind of person who doesn't really care if your privacy is invaded from every direction. This is probably why Diane I both ended up living in Sicily, surrounded by kindred spirits who talk about privacy as a trendy concept, yet come from a culture with a three thousand year tradition of not understanding what it is.

Just to make it clear how far back this goes, we can look to the Romans, whose houses usually had no kitchens or dining rooms because they ate every meal outside at a bar or restaurant. They had no bathrooms because they washed at the public baths, the greatest treat for any ancient Roman. Those inventors of the world's plumbing did not even have toilets at home. In fact, the ancient Romans really put the "public" into public toilets. On a mountain ten minutes from my house in Sicily lie the magnificent ruins of an ancient city with its Roman toilets intact. The Romans had no need for cubicles or walls! They were sociable. They sat close together in a large room, lined with about 16 separate toilet seats set into long benches, discussing current events, literature and digestive issues whilst emptying their bowels. They even shared each other's communal sponges when the time came to wipe, re-adjust their togas and leave the party.

Latin literature, believed to be so cultured by those who haven't read it, is scattered with references to specific people, named and shamed in the community for producing the kinds of smells and sound effects which could ruin one's train of thought in a political debate. Just in case I have left anyone with any residual scepticism about the absence of privacy in Italian tradition – though I doubt it – let me simply add that the Italian language has no word for it. In an Italian-English dictionary, you are offered words which mean intimacy, isolation, or solitude as a translation for privacy. The Italian solution to this linguistic shortfall is simply to use the English word, pronounced very badly with an Italian accent: praaaivasee. Coincidentally – or was it fate? – Diane and I came together through laughing about the complete absence of privacy in Sicily. It has become trendy to put up a show of privacy in Sicily. The Sicilians only want to pretend to be private though. If they achieved actual, real privacy, nobody else would know about it, which would defeat the object completely.

A perfect example is the anecdote I described in my blog "The Dangerously Truthful Diary of a Sicilian Housewife," which caught Diane's eye: 'One of my neighbours, Mrs.

Greenfingers, planted a row of luscious leafy plants along her railings last summer, which created a bit of dappled shade and reduced the x-ray view passers-by had into her living room by about ten percent. Everyone in the street praised her on this wonderful idea for obtaining a bit of privacy. Sorry, I mean praaaivasee. My Mother-in-law liked it more than anyone. Every time she came to visit us, she would stop, bend over and peer through it, looking for a suitable hole through which to check whether the neighbour was at home. The Godmother wanted a good look at her privacy. Mrs. Greenfingers was usually in her garden, peering back out. If not, The Godmother would push some leaves aside and shout out at the top of her voice until she emerged, and responded to The Godmother's friendly greetings and enquiries into her private life. Indeed, the Godmother asked her for gardening advice on cultivating such a succulent screen, as she had decided she thought her newly installed privacy was so enviable they would like to have some praaaaivaseee of her own. Don't run away with the idea my mother-in-law is a particularly prying person. Oh no, everybody peered through that plant screen, all the time.'

Diane responded with her own anecdote about Sicilian privacy. 'I have already blogged about my favourite restaurant in Cianciana, but it is not the only place to get delicious food when you don't want to cook. Even the fast food places make great food. I should clarify "fast food". The menu that sits in the window lists all kinds of wonderful and tasty tempting delights: *verdure grigliate* (grilled vegies), *insalata di polpo* (octopus salad), *insalata di mare* (seafood salad), *tabule' di cuscus freddo* (cold couscous), *pollo allo spiedo* (grilled chicken), *cotoletto alla Milanese* (Milan-style cutlet), *scaloppine ai funghi* (mushroom scaloppini), *arancini* (Sicily's fast food gift from the gods).... But below the mouth-watering list it says: *Ricorda questi piatti solo su ordinazione*!! Remember, these dishes are by order only! So, in other words, fast food in Cianciana means ordering it ahead of time and coming back later to pick it up. One of the dishes they offer is roasted chicken and chips but it is only available on Tuesdays and Sundays and only if you order the day before. Nick and I decided that we would try the chicken and chips one Sunday. As directed by the sign, we ordered on Saturday. On Sunday, about 5pm (which is far too early for the 9pm dinner hour in Sicily) we dropped by the shop to see what time the chicken would be ready. The shop was not open yet, but as we stood outside discussing when we should come back, the neighbour came out on her balcony and shouted down to us in Sicilian, "Are you here for your chicken? Maddelena isn't open yet!".... But the story doesn't end there. The next day, we were heading out to get "*il caffe*'" at our favourite bar. We were stopped by our landlady who asked us how the chicken was. We were a bit bemused as she had not been part of the discussion the previous afternoon. We told her it was wonderful. As we started down the street, we were stopped by one of the ladies from the 'consultation'. "*Come e' andata la cena di pollo*?" she announced to the street. "How was your chicken dinner?" "*Molto bene, grazie.* Very good, thanks." Off we went towards the bar. On the way (it was only two blocks) we were stopped twice more and asked about our chicken and chips.'

 Finding out that the entire town knows what you have

ordered for your dinner before you have even eaten it, and is also bold enough to ask what you thought of it afterwards, is not an experience that everyone would enjoy. Yet it is completely normal for Sicilians and, for a blogger like Diane, nothing to worry about. Indeed, it is simply a sign that Sicilians all have that special character that Diane has: The enthusiasm to make friends out of strangers, even ones you cannot see standing in front of you; that humour and delight in witnessing the eccentricities of your fellow man; and the kind of person who is confident enough to open up about yourself and the things you love to the whole world.

It is another coincidence that Diane's hilarious anecdote about Sicilian-style privacy involved the island's culinary delights, for this is her great passion, and one she shares with almost every man, woman and child on the island. In all cultures, food is a wonderful way to connect and bond with others and, indeed, to bring people from different cultures together.

I am sure you will enjoy this culinary tour of Sicilian culture and food with Diane, and remember this: she doesn't mind if you tell absolutely anyone about this book! In fact, the more the better.

Veronica Di Grigoli
siciliangodmother.com
July 2016

> "Sicilians build things like they will live forever and eat like they will die tomorrow."
> Plato

Preface

Life in Sicily is good. Nick and I made the decision to spend part of our lives in this ancient land for so many reasons. The hot dry summers warm our skins and ease my arthritis. Village life is communal, fun, and supportive. Nick still has many relatives living on the island who welcome us with open arms whenever we come through their towns. The beaches are stunning; the countryside is amazing, and the villages are the very definition of picturesque. But, the most wonderful part of Sicilian life must be the food.

The Tuesday morning market in Cianciana sees me coming home with bags of fragrant sweet peaches from Bivona that have the flavour of the sun; large lemon-shaped cucumbers that are pale green and lightly flavoured; delicious savory and peppery lamb sausages that are the specialty of Cianciana; large fecund oranges from Ribera that drip juice down your chin. And the cheese – oh my goodness the cheese.

Whatever delicacy you decide to try whether picked fresh from the field, bought from the street vendors in Palermo, or served with a flourish in an Ortigian restaurant, you will never regret dipping your toe into the pool that is Sicilian gastronomy.

Table of Contents

Acknowledgements ... 1

Foreword ... 3

Preface ... 8

Chapter One: Under The Sicilian Sun - Anchovies and Oranges ... 11

Chapter Two: Waking Up in Cianciana - Roast Pork with Lemon ... 15

Chapter Three: *Dov'è il Bagno*? - *Panelle* ... 18

Chapter Four: The Bidet in Italy - Sicilian Sausage and Limoncello ... 28

Chapter Five: A Lucky Find - *Arancini* (Fried Stuffed Rice Balls) ... 33

Chapter Six: A Lung and Spleen Sandwich - *Spitini alla Siciliana* (Stuffed Meat Roll-ups) ... 38

Chapter Seven: Open Letter to an (Unnamed) GPS Company - Cold Apples in Red Wine ... 43

Chapter Eight: Eight Things I Miss About Sicily - Maria Cacciato's Completely Easy and Delicious Cookies ... 50

Chapter Nine: Top 10 Crazy Things About Sicily - *Cazzilli* (Fried Potato Pancakes) ... 58

Chapter Ten: Salt - *Caponata* (Eggplant Antipasto) ... 66

Chapter Eleven: Saturday Evening in Cianciana - *Pasta a Picchu Pacchiu* (Spaghetti with Fresh Tomatoes and Garlic) ... 71

Chapter Twelve: Cappuccino in the Afternoon? Must be a Foreigner - Gina and Enza's Easy Coffee Granita ... 75

Chapter Thirteen: Coffee Culture and Italian Names - Franca Tamburello's Amazing Potato Pizza ... 80

Chapter Fourteen: Living Gluten Free in Italy - Mint Beans ... 86

Chapter Fifteen: Telecom Italia and Amazon Duke It Out - Spaghetti with Garlic Sauce ... 92

Chapter Sixteen: Crazy Mice Salad - Sicilian Orange Salad ... 102

Chapter Seventeen: Medieval Monkey Business - Ragusa Lamb Pie ... 108

Chapter Eighteen: *Ferragosto* - Octopus Salad ... 114

Chapter Nineteen: Driving Life's Backroads - Spaghetti with Fried Zucchini ... 119

Chapter Twenty: Gifts from *La Cucina* - Tommaso Caporrimo's Fresh Zucchini & Maristella Mazzara's Pistachio Pasta ... 126

Chapter Twenty-one: The Original Multicultural Society - Sicilian Style Couscous ... 130

Epilogue: Watching the Sun Set Over Sicily ... 138

Index ... 139

Resource List ... 141

Chapter One
Under the Sicilian Sun

One night recently, my husband Nick and I watched Under the Tuscan Sun. This is the third time that I have dragged my patient and long suffering husband to the living room couch to watch this film with me. And it's probably the 10th or 12th time that I have watched the film myself. While *Toscana* may not be the part of Italy that captures my imagination (this is not a dig at Tuscany – it is every bit as romantic and beautiful as the movie portrays), the fictionalized story of Frances Mayes absolutely does capture me and has ever since the film was released in 2003.

At the time that Under the Tuscan Sun hit the theatres I was divorced and had been on my own with my daughter for nine years. I related to Frances in so many ways. I understood the pain of marriage ended by my ex-husband's infidelity. Her struggle to grow beyond the heartache and the loneliness was more familiar than I cared to admit. Watching Frances reinvent herself was exciting; her brief fling with Marcello, while ultimately short-lived, threw me into a daydream that perhaps I too could have a thrilling romantic affair with a dark-haired Italian man. As Frances' wish for a family and a wedding came true, I believed that my wishes could come true as well. And, to make it even more wonderful, it happened against the backdrop of a country that had remained the very definition of romance and magic for me since my teenage years.

While the fictionalized story of Frances Mayes in the film, and her autobiographical account in the book of the same name, made me almost salivate with the desire to pack my bag and hop on the first Alitalia flight out, I had a ten-year-old daughter, a mortgage, and a career that kept me from even considering something like a move to another country. A house in Italy was nothing but a very unlikely daydream.

Fast forward to April 2005. A good friend had convinced me that Internet dating was a good idea. In fact she threatened to make a profile for me if I didn't do it myself. Although the thought of online dating was terrifying, she was right. It was a good idea – in fact it was a great idea. I spent six months going out for coffee, for walks, and to movies with a series of very nice men that I connected with through the dating site that my friend, Wendy, had insisted I join. While all of the men that I met and chatted with online were fun, interesting, kind, etc., there was no spark – that connection that would make me want to see them more than once or twice was not there. Then, one day, early in October, I met someone new for coffee. He was already waiting in the coffee shop and I could see him sitting at a table next to a window. Thick and curly brown hair, gentle grey eyes; I had found my Sicilian romance.

It was clear to us almost immediately that we were a match. We discovered at that first coffee that we were both travellers. We both had seen much of the world, and we were thrilled to find out that we had each visited Sicily at age 13. I was especially excited to hear that topping Nick's list for future travel was a return to Italy. It was, however, the first time we watched Under the Tuscan Sun that the topic of buying a home in Italy came up. A retirement home in Sicily actually seemed to be a possibility.

Today, that Sicilian-Canadian man is my husband and in the summer of 2012 we flew off to Sicily to search for our retirement home in a beautiful village called Cianciana. I look back over the eleven years since we met and I realize that I have indeed, reinvented myself. How appropriate it was then, that we followed the path of Frances Mayes. Like the Frances in the movie, the wishes that I made back in 2003 have all come true. I have a loving husband who is invariably sweet and a daughter who has grown up to be an independent, talented young woman.

Six years ago I returned with Nick and my daughter to Sicily and it was as wonderful as I remembered. And now, Nick and I have a life together in the hills high above the Mediterranean. How could I have imagined, that day back in 1974 when I climbed onto the plane bound for Italy, that the exciting holiday I was about to embark upon would be the first step to a lifetime moving me towards my dream home in romantic Sicily.

"Food is more essential than clothes."
Sicilian proverb

Anchovies and Oranges

Ingredients:

approximately 7 oz. tinned anchovies
1 large orange, squeezed
1 cup green olives, pitted
dried bread crumbs
hot red pepper slices
pine nuts
parsley

1 lemon
dry white wine
olive oil

Directions:

Lightly toast a handful of bread crumbs in a pan.
Rinse anchovies.
Slice lemon into very thin pieces.
Chop parsley and olives.
Arrange a layer of anchovies in a glass oven dish and lay lemon slices on top.
Sprinkle over some pine nuts, chopped parsley and pieces of red pepper and olives and continue until ingredients are used up.
Drizzle with olive oil and a half-cup of wine.
Finish with a layer of bread crumbs.
Bake at 300-350 for 20 minutes. Half way through, douse with the orange juice.

Serves 4.

Chapter Two
Waking up in Cianciana

Nick and I wake at about 3am – jetlag, my least favourite thing about travelling. I try to sleep, toss and turn, try reading, try making up Italian sentences in my head that I might be able to use later. Finally just before 5, Nick and I give up on sleep and rise and dress and climb the stairs to the kitchen.

Nick and I prepare our breakfast with food that our kind neighbours had given us the night before – soft Italian brioche, a chunk of salami cut off a long ring, and plums. Sitting on our *terrazza* we watch the sky change from rose to sand to azure. The ancient stone buildings reflect the colours from the sky and rising sun. They glow with rich Mediterranean morning light. The buildings are a cacophony of angles. An artist would scream with frustration at the different directions of perspective that each of the buildings provide.

Above our heads swallows have taken to the sky. Thousands of them. The air rings with their cries and they swoop so close to us that if I stood at our railing and held out my arms I could touch them.

I take a bite of my plum. The skin yields to my teeth and I can suck all the juice from the inside. Oh such sweetness! Only the skin holds a slight sour flavour making the juice taste even sweeter. It tastes of the orange hills and green orchards we can see from our *terrazza*.

The clock tower strikes 6am. We hear people stirring. A car starts, the *nonna* across the way steps out onto her small *terrazza* to view the morning and to bring in the mop to start her daily cleaning. Voices carry through the clear air. As our friend Joe says of Sicily "It is an island of sanity in a world going mad." How can I possibly add to that?

> **"Who gets married will be happy for a day, who butchers a pig will be happy for a year."**
> **Sicilian Proverb**

Roast Pork With Lemon

Ingredients:

pork chops or pork steaks, enough for four people
1/4 cup of lemon juice
1 1/2 lbs. of new potatoes
olive oil
1 tsp. of orange marmalade per chop or steak
minced garlic to taste
fresh ground pepper
rosemary
2 bay leaves
white flour
sea salt
1 cup of water

Directions:

Preheat oven to 425 degrees.
Slice the potatoes thinly.
Coat the pork with flour.

Heat the oil with the herbs and garlic in the roasting pan.
Place the pork in the pan and sear.
Put one teaspoon of marmalade on each chop or steak.
Add potatoes and salt.
Pour lemon juice over the potatoes and pork.
Roast for 30 minutes.
Add water and roast for another 30 minutes.

Serves 4.

Chapter Three
Dov'è il Bagno?

I am a novice when it comes to the Italian language. As an Italian language learner, I collect words the way some people will collect a fine wine. I will find a word in Italian that fascinates me and I will savour that word, rolling it over my tongue, getting the flavour of it, until I own it and only then can I use it in everyday speech. *Gabinetto* is one of those words. I learned this one from my husband who grew up using it at home. Try saying it.... *gabinetto. Gaaaa binnn ettttooooo.* It just rolls off your tongue. For those of you who speak Italian, you are probably giggling or rolling your eyes at my fascination with this word. For those of you who don't speak Italian, this very smooth and romantic sounding word does not have a particularly smooth or romantic sound in English. What does it mean? Well, not to put too fine a point on it, it means toilet.

I have, believe it or not, often thought about public toilets in Sicily and they were a constant topic of conversation when my husband and my daughter and I first travelled together to Italy back in 2010. What was so interesting about a toilet, you may ask? Well, here are my top ten topics of toilet conversation (how is that for alliteration?).

Number One
Toilet Seats

For some reason, public toilets in Italy frequently are *senza* (without) toilet seats. Actually, I have read that it is because no self-respecting Italian with a normal amount of hygienic concern would ever sit on a public toilet, therefore no need to shell out the extra euros for a toilet seat. I don't know if this is true or not, but it may be. In any case, this is an issue for someone like me who has knee problems, depending on the height of the toilet. What to do? Well, I also have a normal amount of hygienic concern so I have been known to take a wad of toilet tissue, put a dollop of liquid soap on it and actually wash the porcelain rim before carefully placing my derriere on the *gabinetto*. Sometimes, however, there is no soap, so I have laid out the toilet tissue along the edge of the porcelain so that there is a "barrier" between my pristine bottom and the toilet's edge.

Number Two
Toilet Paper Part 1

One day, I was in a public toilet that had a little sign that had been translated into English. "Please do not put paper in toilet." What? Don't put paper in the toilet? What are you supposed to do with it? Looking around, I noticed a small garbage can next to the toilet filled with toilet tissue. 'Ewwww' was my first reaction. But then, as I got to know Sicily and it's plumbing and water issues better, it began to make much more sense. Coming from the west coast of Canada, the oldest still-standing house was built in 1852. Most buildings are 50 years old or less and therefore have plumbing that is similarly aged. The pipes are big and the plumbing is up to code. In Sicily, many many buildings are 100 years old or more and the pipes are tiny and plumbing code is just non-existent. An example of this was when our bathroom was leaking through the ceiling below. We had the tub ripped out and beneath the floor were teeny-tiny rusted out pipes wrapped in asbestos. Another problem is water volume. Canada has more fresh water than any other country in the world. In fact, we have more lakes in Canada than the whole rest of the world combined! Sicily, on the other hand, at least in our corner of Sicily, has an average rainfall in the summer of zero. Yup, you read it. No rain all summer for the most part. This means that the extra water needed to flush big wads of toilet paper just aren't available. So, paper in many places, goes in the garbage not in the toilet. I will say, however, that I think if your deposit is, how shall I say it, not just liquid, no one expects that toilet tissue to go anywhere but in the toilet. This leads me to top ten #3

Number Three
Flushing the Toilet

In Canada, the variety of flushers on a toilet is very narrow. The tank sits at the back of the toilet, the flusher is either a handle on the side of the tank or a button, or two buttons on the top. On very new and fancy public toilets, there might be sensors that flush as soon as you stand. In Italy, the variety of ways to flush the toilet seems to be endless. There are, of course, flushers that are the same as in Canada. But then, some toilets have tanks that are way above the head of the user and the flusher is actually a string with a handle that you pull. Sometimes I have seen a foot pedal on the floor or a button on the wall. Once I came across a button on the bathroom wall that had to be pushed before you could depress the lever on the top of the toilet tank. And every now and then I will come across one that stumps me. One summer, I used a public toilet in a bar at a big *festa*. There was a line up before and after me. After I finished I looked for the flusher. No button, handle or lever on the tank. No pedal on the floor. No button on the wall that I could see. What to do? I couldn't stay in there forever as there was a long line outside waiting, so I did the only thing I could do. I left without flushing. The woman after me, as I stood washing my hands, started into the little toilet "room", did a double take and stopped to give me a very dirty look. Then she reached up and flipped a switch that I had assumed was the light switch. Toilet flushed. That was a new one on me.

Number Four
Toilet Paper Part 2

Now, toilet paper, in my mind, is a fairly basic necessity when one is using a toilet. In Italy, however, I have regularly come across public toilets with no toilet paper and no sign that there ever was toilet paper. Not a stray square on the floor. No empty cardboard tube. In fact, the toilet paper holder may be dusty and clearly unused! Carrying a little package of tissues is fairly important. I came across this same problem when I lived in Japan where NO public toilets have paper. The solution? Businesses often pay young women to stand at train stations and hand out small tissue packages with their company's advertising on the outside. Problem solved. Sadly, no such system exists in Italy which leads me to my fifth point.

Number Five
Toilet Stalls

Most women in North America, I would venture to say, have had the experience of being in a toilet stall and realizing there was no paper. No problem. Just check for feet in the next stall and ask the woman there to pass you a bit of paper. We are all sisters. We've all been there. In Italy, many public toilets are stand alones. One room that often contains not only the toilet but the sink as well. No understanding woman in the next stall to ask. When there are a number of stalls, they often go right to the floor. There is no space underneath the separating wall so there is no way to check for feet. In some ways, I applaud this privacy but it does make it difficult to say: "*Mi scusi. Mi puoi passare un po'di carta igienica?*"

Number Six
Pay Toilets

The whole pay toilet thing came as a huge shock to me. I remember pay toilets being outlawed in British Columbia in the early 1970s and I hadn't seen a pay toilet since then. Pay toilets still exist in Europe, including in Italy. Train stations, in particular, will have pay toilets with an attendant who is there to make sure you can get the change you need to enter, which is a good thing, because sometimes the cost of a toilet is a very odd number indeed. I was in Palermo Central Station one hot summer day after a two-hour bus ride from Cianciana. My teeth were swimming, as they say, and I made a beeline for the big WC sign. When I got there, I discovered that the cost was 80 *centesimi*. I had in my wallet lots of €1, €2 and 50 *centesimi* coins and one little 20 *centesimi* coin but not a single 10 *centesimi* coin! The attendant took pity on my poor desperate face and let me in for 70. Some public toilets are the ridiculous price of 75 *centesimi*. Not ridiculous because it is expensive, but ridiculous because no one ever seems to have the 5 *centesimi* coin in their purse or pocket! The only place I have ever been given 5 *centesimi* is in the grocery store and rarely at that. Another place I have had to pay, and pay dearly, is at the beach. One of our favourite beaches is Eraclea Minoa. There are several entrances to that beach with numerous bars and no public toilets. Even though, as I understand it, Italian law says that no commercial establishment can refuse someone the right to use the toilet, customer or no, this isn't always the practice. At the bar near the entrance we often use to Minoa, there is a sign on the door to the washroom: €3 to use the washroom if you are not a customer. I generally go in and buy a bottle of water for €1 and then ask for the key. This leads us to…

Number 7
Cleanliness

The advantage of pay toilets is that they are usually kept clean and stocked. I have seen, however a huge range of hygiene in public toilets in Italy from absolutely shiny and pristine to so disgusting I crossed my legs and waddled off to look for another toilet. I will say, however, that my experience is that public toilets in Italy are generally cleaner than public toilets in North America, particularly gas station toilets, which, I think, goes back to the Italian concern for personal hygiene. This, of course, leads us to…

Number 8
Bidets

I think bidets deserve a whole chapter unto themselves however I will mention them briefly here. Occasionally I will see a bidet in a bar or restaurant. This is usually because the place was a home at one time and they haven't bothered to remove the bidet. All hotels and B&Bs must have a bidet. For North Americans and Brits, this may be surprising but it is the norm for continental Europeans. The first time I saw a bidet I had no clue what it was for and even when I discovered its purpose, I had to look up on YouTube how to use one. Okay, I know you European types out there are reading this going, "Are you kidding? Isn't it obvious?" Well, now that I know, yes.

Number 9
Hand washing

Like the flush issue, public toilet sinks have a wide variety of ways to turn the water off and on. There are, of course, the normal taps with handles for hot and cold. Note here, just because a handle indicates the water is either hot or cold doesn't mean it will be. Old buildings (our house included) will sometimes have hot where the cold is and cold where the hot should be. Sometimes you can turn the water on by pressing a lever on the floor. Sometimes you will be lucky and there will be a modern sensor and you don't have to do anything but wave your hands under the tap. There may or may not be soap so a little bottle of liquid soap tucked into your purse along with the tissues is not a bad idea. And gentlemen of North America, Italian men often carry their "murse (man-purse)" with them. There will be no question about your masculinity if you carry one in Italy. Finally, again, there may or may not be paper towels or a hot (warm) air dryer so carrying a little hanky in your purse or murse is a good idea.

Number 10
Best Places To Find a Toilet You Can Use

Public toilets that are not in a commercial site like a bar or a restaurant, are few and far between in Italy. The best places to find a toilet are:

- bars – if you are in a small town, this is your best bet. You may have to buy something but *il caffè* is usually less than a euro and well worth the expense if you really need a washroom;
- train stations and bus stations;
- department stores and large hotels – if you are in a city, you can usually use these for free…but not always. If they have an attendant, you are expected to tip;
- libraries and museums;
- big chain fast food joints – again, these are mostly in the larger cities. You won't find a McDonalds in a little Sicilian village;
- churches – you have to ask and there is an unstated expectation that you will leave a few coins in the donation box.

In our many conversations about public toilets, Nick and I developed what we call the C.B.R.S. or the Cacciato Bathroom Rating Scale. Perhaps this will catch on like the Trip Advisor stickers you see in the windows of so many establishments.

A bathroom gets 1 point for each of the following:

- A toilet seat. You would not believe how many bathrooms have toilets with no toilet seat or half a toilet seat. Yes, I said half a toilet seat. I don't mean that the seat is missing the cover that comes down – I mean half the seat part is missing. Hard to imagine how a toilet can be so abused as to lose half its seat but there you go.

- Toilet paper. Always carry tissue with you. Toilet paper is not a given.
- A clear way to flush the toilet. I am not kidding. There are more ways to flush a toilet in Italy that I have ever experienced in any other country. Handles on the side or top of the toilet. A chain to pull. A button on the wall beside, behind or on the opposite wall to the toilet. A push pedal on the floor. An automatic flush (these are rare). And then sometimes you just can't find any way to flush at all. Or if you do find the button, handle, lever, pedal and use it... nothing happens. I've experienced all of these.
- A clear way to turn on the water in the sink. See above.
- Soap in the dispenser.
- A way to dry your hands – paper in the dispenser or a blow dryer that actually works.
- Clean. Definitely not a given.

"A contented stomach, a forgiving heart; an empty
stomach forgives nothing."
Sicilian proverb

Panelle (Chickpea Fritters)

Ingredients:

½ cup of chickpea (garbanzo bean) flour
1 cup of water
1 tbsp. chopped fresh parsley, oregano or basil
salt and pepper to taste
olive oil
vegetable oil (for frying)

Directions:

Prepare a wooden or stone (granite or marble) surface by covering thinly with olive oil.
Pour water into a saucepan and whisk in the flour, salt and pepper and the chopped herbs.
Heat the mixture on a medium heat, stirring continuously for about 15 minutes until it has thickened and separated from the sides of the saucepan.
Scoop out the mixture onto the flat, oiled surface and cover with plastic wrap.
Role out very thinly (about 1/16th of an inch) with a rolling pin while the mixture is still hot.
Let the thin mixture cool.
Remove the wrap and then cut into small rectangular fritters.
Pour vegetable oil into a frying pan to a depth of about 1 inch.

Heat oil until quite hot but not smoking.
Put the fritters into the oil and fry until golden on one side and then flip and fry on the other.
Drain on paper towel and serve while still hot.

Makes 10 fritters

Chapter Four
The Bidet in Italy
Or
What the Heck is This Toilet-looking Thing?

    I am such a Canadian. I was born and raised in Canada and other than a three-year stint teaching English in Japan, until we bought our house in Cianciana, I only ever lived in Canada.

    What is a Canadian like? Well, many of the stereotypes are true and some are not. I do say "sorry" all the time but I rarely say "eh". Typical conversation in Canada:

Two people are walking through The Hudson Bay department store. Canadian #1 bumps into Canadian #2 by accident while looking at winter coats.

Canadian #2: Oh, sorry.
Canadian #1: Sorry.
Canadian #2: Are you looking at these coats?
Canadian #1: Yeah, since it's August, I thought I'd better get a new winter coat before the snow comes.
Canadian #2: Sorry, I hate to say this, but I bought that coat last winter and it wasn't very warm. Sorry.
Canadian #1: Really? My daughter bought this last year and she said it was great. Sorry.
Canadian #2: Oh, sorry. I don't want to contradict your daughter. Sorry.
Canadian #1: Oh, sorry. No it's fine.
Canadian #2: Well, I should get going. Sorry. It was nice to chat with you, eh.
Canadian #1: Oh, yeah. Sorry, I didn't mean to take up your time. Thanks for the advice, eh. Bye.

Notice all the sorrys? We really do this - maybe not quite that much. Also notice that there were only 2 "ehs"? Canadians do sometimes say "eh" at the end of sentences but not as much as the stereotype would lead you to believe. Oh, and sorry for all the hyperbole.

What else is typically Canadian? Well, many Canadians do like maple syrup and it is available pretty much ubiquitously. My husband, Nick, loves maple syrup and I think if we ran out and didn't replace it immediately, he might actually cry. Not a pretty sight to see a grown man cry over lack of maple syrup so I make sure we always have some in the house.

Addendum: Nick wants me to say that he has NEVER cried over maple syrup in his life and that last paragraph was another example of hyperbole. Sorry.

Another thing about Canadians is that we haven't got a clue about bidets. Bidets don't exist in Canada. I have heard of non-Europeans using bidets for all kinds of things other than their actual intended use. Here are a few:

1. Pet drinking fountain,
2. Foot washing centre,
3. Leg shaving sink,
4. Bath for babies,
5. Beer cooler,
6. Storage for wet umbrellas,
7. Place to keep plants,
8. Station for washing underwear and other delicates,
9. Bed for the cat,
10. Water play station for the kids, and
11. Goldfish bowl

The first time I saw a bidet I could not for the life of me figure out what it was for. Was it a different kind of toilet? If so, the drain seemed pretty small. Was it a kind of sink? Then why was it shaped like a toilet and at seat height and why was there also a normal sink? What the heck was it? I asked Nick and he informed me that it was a bidet and it was for washing your "bits". Okay. I could understand that. I had come across a few high tech toilets in Japan that had shooting water and fans to dry you. But, those were toilets.

How did you use the bidet? I mean, which way did you sit? If you sat the same direction as the toilet, then how do you reach the tap? (Italian bidets are a little different than other places in Europe as they don't have water that 'shoots' up at you – it's more like a sink that you sit over.) If you sit the other way, you have to completely remove your pants and underwear otherwise it's impossible to sit and that seemed a bit excessive to me. And, I didn't see any cloths. Did you use your hands to wash? And which bits were you supposed to focus on? The front bits or the back bits? So many questions! Well, all I can say is…Thank you YouTube! I found hundreds of videos to help. So, for all those Canadians (and Americans) out there who have never seen a bidet, just have a quick search on YouTube for "how to use a bidet" and all answers will be revealed.

You're welcome and… sorry.

"You can't have meat without the bone."
Sicilian proverb

Sicilian Sausage and Limoncello

Ingredients:

1 – 1 ½ lbs. of Italian sausage in a coil.
1 ½ cups of limoncello
2 tbsp preserved lemon peel, cut into small pieces
non-stick spray

Directions:

Preheat oven to 350F.
Line a round baking dish with aluminum foil and spray with non-stick spray.
Place the sausage coil in the dish, tuck lemon pieces between the rings and pour the limoncello over the sausage, making sure that the limoncello pools in the joins between the rings of the sausage.
Cover with aluminum foil and place in the oven.
Bake for 45 minutes.
Remove the foil and bake for another 20 minutes until brown on top.

Serves 8.

Chapter Five
A Lucky Find

One of the things that I love about Sicily (and I think this is true about all of Italy) is how often one can find an amazing gastronomical delight completely by accident. Now, not every meal is a gastronomical delight… the time our friends invited us to a picnic and served barbequed sheep's testicles comes to mind. But, sometimes Nick and I will stop in at a bar or restaurant that is just a little hole in the wall and will discover something wonderful that keeps us coming back. The Bar Zamenhoff is one of those places.

Ribera is a town about 20-30 minutes from Cianciana (depending if you drive like most Sicilians, or if you drive like an old man in a Fiat Panda like I do). Every Thursday morning is market day and the market in Ribera is a good one – big (for a town rather than a city), busy and lots to choose from. One day, after the market, Nick and I were looking for somewhere to get a cold drink and something to eat, preferably with air conditioning. We wandered down the street from the market, about 5 minutes away to the *Piazza* Zamenhoff and found the Bar Zamenhoff. From the outside it looked much like any other bar, but when we wandered inside, we found what has become our favourite place to stop in Ribera.

Ribera is a town full of dichotomies. It is not a pretty town by any stretch of the imagination. In fact if, on my first visit to Italy, I had been dropped into the middle of Ribera, I would have left Italy in disgust. It is dusty, dirty and full of truly ugly modern-esque buildings. Having said this, there is much that brings me to Ribera. The market I have already mentioned. I love the little market in Cianciana, but the market in Ribera is larger and has much more selection and unlike the market in Sciacca (which is larger still) you do not have to walk up so many hills that you get a nosebleed from the altitude. Ribera also has the appliance store that all the expats from Cianciana visit. The owner, whose name I do not know, is very happy to welcome us with slow and clearly pronounced Italian and he delivers for free to Cianciana. Lidl and Eurospin are both in Ribera and are supermarkets that carry items we can't get in our local green grocers or butchers. Ribera also specializes in the wonderful sweet oranges that are in season in the early spring. And Ribera has Bar Zamenhoff.

Anyone who has spent much time in Sicily will know about *arancini* – those amazing fried rice balls that can make one weep they are so yummy. My favourite *arancino* by far, however, is the pesto and shrimp *arancino* that they make in the Bar Zamenhoff. It is… phenomenal. But the Bar Zamenhoff is much more than that.

The Six Reasons I Love the Bar Zamenhoff (beyond their great *arancini*):

1. Air conditioning. They have good air conditioning, which, after a long hot morning at the market, is so appreciated.
2. Cleanliness. This bar is clean! Not to give the impression that most Sicilian bars are not – but the Zamenhoff is really clean. In fact, on the Cacciato Bathroom Rating Scale, the Bar Zamenhoff gets a seven out of seven.
3. Courtesy. The staff at this bar is invariably courteous and helpful. They have always waited patiently as I stumbled over my inadequate Italian. They bring glasses of water (with lemon!) to the table without being asked. They smile and say "*Grazie*" in a sincere tone. And if you speak to Angelo, the owner, he will greet you with a grin and a handshake.
4. Interesting things to look at all over the bar. The décor may not make it into *Better Homes and Gardens*, but Angelo has covered the walls with so many interesting pictures and hangings that there is always something to look at and comment on as you munch away at your lunch.
5. The television. So many bars put up a television on the wall to play music videos and then blast the music out so loudly that you cannot have a conversation. Bar Zamenhoff has the requisite television set to whichever of the music video stations is the preferred one, however the volume is low enough, even when sitting under the speakers, you can have a conversation comfortably.
6. And finally, the most important one - food. I've already mentioned the *arancini*, but they also have many other delicious pastries, *panini*, pizza, and truly yummy

deserts including beautiful *gelato*, *granita* and cakes.

"Do not be sweet lest you be eaten. Do not be sour lest you be shunned."
Sicilian proverb

Arancini

Ingredients:

2 cups cooked white short-grain (arborio) rice
½ cup grated Parmesan cheese
3 medium eggs
1 cup grated mozzarella and 2 thin slices of sandwich ham
or 1 cup of pesto and ¼ cup of cooked crevette (tiny shrimp)
1 cup bread crumbs, either Italian bread crumbs or regular
bread crumbs with dried oregano, basil and parsley added to

taste
1 tbsp. of pasta sauce
Oil, for frying

Directions:

Pour the oil into a large heavy saucepan and turn heat on medium-high. It should be 4-5 inches in depth.
Place the cooked rice in a large bowl and let sit to cool. Stir the rice occasionally.
Add the parmesan, one egg and pasta sauce to the rice and mix with your hands until the mixture is well combined.
Chop the ham slices into little pieces.
Take a small handful of rice and form into a ball. Squeeze the ball to make sure it sticks together.
Using your thumb, create an indentation into the centre of the rice ball.
Fill half way with mozzarella and ham or pesto and shrimp and then fill the indentation with more rice. Squeeze the ball together again.
Continue making rice balls until the rice has been used up.
Beat the two eggs in a bowl and pour the bread crumbs into a second bowl.
Dip each rice ball into the egg mixture and then into the bread crumbs, rolling it around to make sure it is completely covered.
When the oil is hot, place two rice balls in the oil and wait until they are a golden colour.
Remove with a slotted spoon and place on kitchen paper to soak up excess oil.
Repeat until all the rice balls are cooked.
Eat immediately but be careful - the inside might be quite hot!

This makes 8 *arancini*.

Chapter Six
A Lung and Spleen Sandwich

One summer, Nick and I decided that it was high time to get past the terror of the extreme chaos that is Palermo and take ourselves into the capital city to see what all the hoopla was about.

"Oh, you can't miss Palermo!" said our family and

friends.

"What makes Palermo so great?" we asked.

"Well, it's, you know...Palermo." came the supremely helpful response.

So, we found ourselves one very hot and sticky afternoon touring Palermo. We stumbled upon the *Fontana della Vergogna* in the *Piazza Pretoria* quite by happy accident. We both enjoyed the lovely sculptures in this quiet corner of what is otherwise a crazy city. The *piazza* is closed in on three sides by the Praetorian, Bonocore, and Bordonaro Palaces as well as the Church of Saint Catherine. In the centre is a lovely fountain surrounded by statues: some imposing, some whimsical, some playful and some somber but all beautiful and all very, very nude. The name, *Fontana della Vergogna*, translates to the Fountain of Shame. I have heard differing reasons that the fountain was named thusly. Some say it was because of the nudity and some say the fountain was named for corruption in the early Palermo government however, my favourite story is this: shortly after the fountain and statues were placed in *Piazza Pretoria*, the nuns that lived in the convent across the street would walk by shouting "Shame! Shame!" until one night they crept out of their convent with chisels and hammers and removed all of the 'naughty bits'. I cannot say if this is true or not, but it does make a good story.

One of our truly memorable moments in Palermo was when we came across a street vendor cooking up what appeared to be a Sicilian version of a sloppy joe called *pani ca' meusa*. The street chef scooped a generous portion of stewed meat onto a soft bun, wrapped it in a paper napkin and handed it to us. We shared the sandwich and agreed that it was quite delicious. Nick asked the food cart proprietor what kind of meat was in the sandwich.

"Spleen and lung." came the reply.

"Pardon?" Nick spluttered.

"Spleen and lung." our chef answered, this time with a grin that widened when he saw the greenish tinge replacing Nick's healthy tan. It was obviously not the first time he had had that conversation.

"How the hell does someone come up with the idea of a spleen and lung sandwich?" I asked Nick later.

"I don't know – I just know I don't need to have another one." he replied.

The story behind *pani ca' meusa* goes back to the Arab era between mid 800 CE and 1072 CE. The Arabs were good administrators and tolerant leaders. Palermo flourished, and in the atmosphere of religious tolerance of the time, a strong and economically successful Jewish community grew. Many of the successful Jewish citizens would hire Sicilian servants. Because they kept kosher homes, certain parts of the animals could not be eaten and Sicilians, being the frugal people that they are, took home the kidneys, spleens and lungs and from that a whole cuisine blossomed that is seen today in the street food carts of Palermo.

"It was not such beautiful parsley, and then the cat went and peed on it."
Sicilian proverb

Stuffed Meat Rolls (Spitini alla Siciliana)

Ingredients:

8 frozen pork cutlets, chicken breasts, lamb chops, or small steaks
4-6 green onions chopped
4 minced cloves of garlic
¼ cup cooked and crumbled bacon
¾ cup seasoned bread crumbs
1/3 cup pecorino or romano cheese if you like a sharp flavour or caciocavallo cheese if you like a milder flavour
1/8 cup chopped fresh parsley or basil or oregano depending on your preference
½ tsp. salt
½ tsp. pepper
1 can of tomato sauce
non-stick spray

Directions:

Lay a sheet of wax paper on a cutting board.
Place your piece(s) of meat on the wax paper and cover it with a second piece of wax paper.
Using a kitchen mallet, hammer on the meat until the pieces are about 1/8" – ¼" thin. With the beef, pork, and lamb you can hammer fairly hard. With the chicken, just tap two or

three times.

Mix the remaining ingredients together in a medium-sized bowl. If the mixture is too liquid, add extra bread crumbs.

Put one spoonful on the end of each piece of meat.

Roll up the stuffing mixture and secure using a toothpick.

Line a baking sheet with aluminum foil, spray with the non-stick spray, and place all the meat rolls on the baking sheet.

Place the baking sheet on the middle shelf in the oven.

Set the broiler on high.

After about 20 minutes, when they are starting to brown, turn the rolls.

Return the rolls to the oven and broil for another 15 minutes or until brown.

This makes 8 rolls.

Chapter Seven
Open Letter To An (Unnamed) GPS Company

Dear (Unnamed GPS) Executives;

WTF!

Now, don't get me wrong. Our GPS has been invaluable here in Sicily. There have been many places we never would have found without it. But seriously.

WTF.

Yesterday, Nick – my navigator and darling hubby – and I left Noto, a fair-sized city, to return to our new home in Cianciana, a town a comfortable 30 minute drive from Sciacca, the largest city in our province of Agrigento. The GPS assured us, on the screen, that we would be home in 3 ½ hours. Pretty much what we had expected. The first 1 ½ hours were smooth sailing. The *autostrade* (freeways), all over Italy, are superb, including the ones in Sicily. A quick jaunt to Siracusa (or Syracuse for you non-Italian types) and we were on the *autostrada* to Catania; an easy switch and we were on the *autostrada* in the direction of Palermo, Sicily's largest city. I fully expected that we would take the turn off to Caltanisetta, a city in the centre of Sicily that has good roads taking you to almost every point on the island. From there south to the city of Agrigento and along the well paved, albeit windy mountain road to Cianciana. Piece o' cake, right? Oh no, my high-powered GPS provider friends. Here is how it went.

The turn off to Caltanisetta whizzed past us as we drove along the *autostrada*, going under the speed limit at 120 km/hour. That would be 80 mph for those unaccustomed to the metric system. We had set our GPS to speak in the voice of a Canadian male. We didn't want to be confused by a British, Australian, South African, American or any other English-speaking accent while driving at high speeds. So, as we drove past the exit for Caltinasetta, our Canadian GPS buddy was oddly silent. But, we trusted him! And so we continued on for another 2 or 3 exits until our GPS announced, "Get off the highway!!! Get offffff! Get offffff!!!!!" No, I am not exaggerating. This is exactly what he said. And that is exactly what I did – hitting the brakes and swerving off the highway at the last minute. Why at the last minute? Because that was all the time that GPS guy gave me to turn.

We followed his instructions through several small towns, along winding roads. Winding roads are *normale* in Sicily. This is an island full of volcanic mountains and river valleys. And while Sicily is also covered with small back country roads, lanes and goat paths, what we didn't expect, when there was a perfectly good highway almost all the way to Cianciana, was to be sent along progressively narrower and narrower roads, lanes and goat paths.

We drove through villages so small that to call them a village was an exaggeration of the highest order. Sometimes GPS guy, very soon to be known as "The Asshole", would call me a "doofus" or "the dork on the steering wheel". Okay, I know what you are thinking. Perhaps I am a doofus or a dork on the steering wheel.

Well, oh GPS provider execs, I would like to see you make your way through a 6 lane traffic circle, battling 30 or 40 cars, and exit immediately after without bumping or scratching someone's shiny, beautiful Alfa Romeo or Lamborghini because I have done that. Or could you wind your way through a herd of cattle while the bull stood waving his very long horns at you menacingly? Because I have done that too. In fact, it was GPS guy, AKA the Asshole, who was the doofus. Frequently we would be travelling along a road and the Asshole would tell us to turn right in 200 metres. Oh, did I say turn right? What he actually said was "Turn right-left in …200… metres." What the hell? Turn right-left? Which was it??? Thank gawd Nick was looking at the screen and could tell me which one the Doofus in the GPS actually meant. If I had been on my own I would probably, today, be stuck in the middle of a field surrounded by sheep being oogled by a shepherd who hadn't seen another person, much less a woman, in weeks. I shudder.

On the subject of turning right or left, Doofus would, on occasion, tell us to turn. What was the problem? There was no turn. Not right, not left, nowhere. "Oh", you say, "Did you update your maps of Europe?" And I answer, "Doesn't freaking matter." You see, not only was there no turn, there had never been any turn. In fact, on some of those turns, if I had listened to The A.H., I would have driven off a cliff. Something that I seriously considered doing, á la Thelma and Louise, as the afternoon turned into evening turned into night.

Let me pause to wax lyrical about some of these "roads" down which the "Dork in the GPS" sent us. You may think that I am joking about the goat paths. We drove down paths that 20 km/hour (12 mph) was a breakneck speed. There were holes in the road that had goat skeletons at the bottom! An inch one way or another and we would have been, to quote John Cleese, "pushing up the daisies" or "joining the choir invisible". In fact, we would each have been "a NON parrot!" had we been parrots to start out with. On one of these paths we passed a shepherd who literally stopped in his tracks, mouth wide open, and watched, in amazement, as we inched by.

This morning, when I arose, after giving some truly heartfelt prayers of thanks that we had actually made it home, I looked at the map of Sicily. I managed to get a rough idea of our route from the map. We had taken roads that were not just secondary roads. They were not the roads that were marked as smaller than secondary roads. They were so small that they did not exist on our quite detailed map of Sicily. And all of this I could have lived with but for the following. The Dorky, Stupid-head Doofus of an Asshole of a GPS guy kept changing his freaking mind! We would turn where we were told to turn and he would say "Oh my gawd, you've gone the wrong way! Turn...the car...around!" AAARRRRRGGGGHHHHH!!!!!!!!!!!!

Way up in the mountains, not an inhabited building, or a vehicle or person to be seen as we drove along the goat-paths, we watch the sun go down behind the mountains. Beautiful sunset. But do you know how many streetlights can be found on goat-paths in the mountains? NONE!!!! So we went from this...

to this...

in the space of about 2 ½ minutes. You can imagine this slowed my driving down just a tad. And there was another thing. Agrigento, in the heat of the summer, is prone to fires in the mountain fields. The Poopy-headed Doofus of a GPS guy directed us to not one, but two fires that we had to find our way around. In the dark. You see, the 3½ hour trip, which had started about 5pm, went on not 4 hours. Not 5 hours. Not even 6 hours. It went on for 6 ½ hours. SIX AND A HALF HOURS!

You see, GPS executives, we really didn't start out from Noto with a plan to be the SS Minnow. We (I suppose we being the Skipper and Gilligan) didn't want to be off on the 3 ½ hour cruise only to be shipwrecked without even the Professor, Thurston Howell III, Mrs. Howell, Ginger and MaryAnn for company! (Although I suspect my husband would have forgiven you much faster if you had provided Ginger and MaryAnn as travelling companions).

I just want to say, come to Sicily. Take our GPS. In fact, we would even put you up in our house! Come here, and I dare you – **I dare you** – to drive from Noto to Cianciana using only your GPS for directions.

Sincerely,

The Dork on the Steering Wheel.

"There is no table without wine nor sermon without Augustine."
Sicilian Proverb

Cold Apples in Red Wine

Ingredients:

4 apples, pared and quartered
1 cup dry red wine
½ cup sugar
sprig of fresh mint
¼ cup vanilla yogurt, ice cream, whipped cream, or cream

Directions:

In a saucepan, bring the wine and the sugar to a slow boil. Add apples, reduce heat and simmer for about 10 minutes. Using a slotted spoon, remove apples and place in a serving dish.
Continue to simmer the wine/sugar mixture until it is about half the volume and is syrupy.
Remove from heat and set aside to cool.
Pour syrup over apples.
Place fresh mint on top

You can serve this, warm or cold, with cream, whipped cream, yogurt or ice cream or just eat as is.

Serves 4.

Chapter Eight
Eight Things I Miss When We Are Away From Sicily

One of my favourite bloggers from Sicily, Rochelle Del Borrello, has posted on her blog, her list of "Ten Ways To Tell You've Been Living In Sicily Too Long". She's not alone. Veronica di Grigoli posted a similar entry on her blog *The Dangerously Truthful Diary of a Sicilian Housewife* and Jennifer Avventura wrote about "The Forty Ways You Know You've Been Living in Sardinia Too Long" in *My Sardinian Life*.

Nick and I haven't been living in Sicily nearly long enough to write a similar post, but, instead, I offer the "Eight Things I Miss When We Are Away From Cianciana".

1. One of the things that I miss the most from our house in Cianciana is the view. Our stunning 180 degrees of beautiful Sicilian mountainside, the charming houses in the old part of the town, and our glimpse of the Mediterranean off to the south calls me every day that we

are away. The first thing that I do when we get back to our home is to climb the stairs to the kitchen, open the door to the terrazza and then stand at the rail taking in the view that I have missed so much.

2. In the morning, I get up early – well, early for me in Cianciana – and walk down to the fruit and veggie shop to by fresh peaches or a melon and some pecorino cheese, into the butcher to buy salami, and then I walk up to the street above ours and buy fresh, warm Italian bread for Nick. While I am doing that, Nick makes the espresso and when I get home, he and I sit on our *terrazza*, drinking our coffee and eating our breakfast and enjoying our view before the day gets too hot.

3. Every day, Sicilians partake in a centuries old practice that I find to be the utmost of civilized customs. This is a custom that Nick and I have embraced and indulge in while we are in Sicily and wish we could indulge in while we are in Canada. This most wonderful of customs is the afternoon siesta. From about 1:00 – 4:00, all businesses shut down and everyone heads home for lunch and a nap. Many parts of Italy are humid in the summer, but Cianciana lies in Agrigento, a region that is known for hot, dry summers. I love to lie down and feel the heat, soft and dry, envelop me as I drift off to sleep for an hour or two. In Palermo, the summers are humid and the same nap would leave me sweaty and sticky but in Cianciana, I wake up warm and refreshed, ready for the afternoon.

4. Every Tuesday morning in Cianciana, and every Thursday morning in nearby Ribera, there is a market. I LOVE shopping in Sicilian markets. There are a myriad of stalls with everything you can possibly imagine that you could possibly need plus a whole lot that you don't need but

are still interesting to poke through. Having people over for dinner and don't know what to make? Ask the fishmonger what's good and how he would make it. After politics, I think discussing food – eating it and how to make it is the second most debated topic of conversation. Looking for a new shirt or dress to wear out in the evening? Rows upon rows of the latest styles at rock bottom prices are there for you to peruse. Need something for the kitchen? Bathroom? New curtains? Sheets for the bed? New light fixtures? Furniture? We have bought all of these from the market. I leave Nick to run his errands (he's not as fond of shopping as I am) and I am in heaven wandering up and down the alleyways that make up the market.

5.   Gelato. What else can I say? Oh, except, gelato in a sweet bun. I love Sicily.

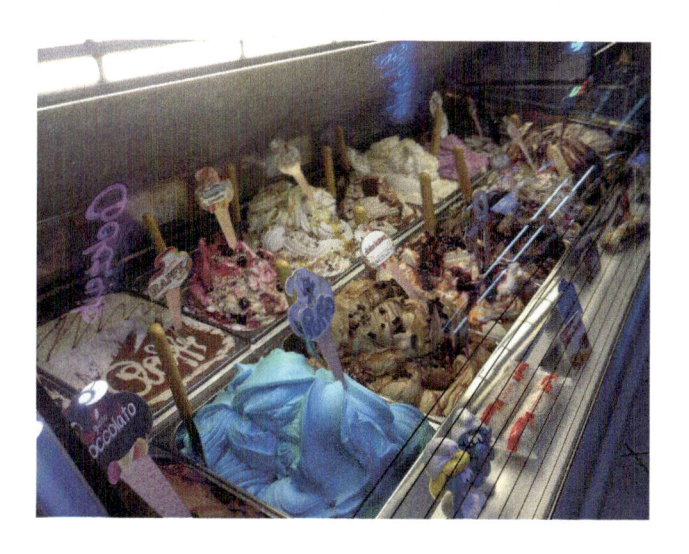

6.   One of the things that I really hoped to find in Sicily

was community. Nick and I have been living in the same neighbourhood in Canada for years – nine on my part and twenty-two on Nick's. On our Canadian street, I have met four sets of neighbours, actually been in the homes of one and I rarely see or speak to the other three. In Cianciana, we met our next-door neighbours even before we had decided to buy the house. The people in our Sicilian neighbourhood have had us over for dinner, for coffee, to their homes in the country. We have met their children, their parents, their grandchildren. Even our friends who are *stranieri* (foreigners) we see and visit more often than our friends in Canada. It is not possible to spend time in our small Sicilian village without making connections with the people there. Every year before departing for Cianciana, I am excited at the thought of once again sitting out in the evening with Guiseppe, Anna and Antonio from next door, or Anna down the street, or dropping by to visit Enzo and his wife Enza in the street above. I love hanging out with Pat and her kitties, or discussing the new renos on Diane's house in town and Doug and Ian's house out in the country, or sitting and having coffee with Sav in the Clock Tower Café which invariable brings fascinating conversation. I love sharing the view from Linda and Bruno's new home on the other side of the island, or Lynda and German's new villa down the road from our piece of land. I always look forward to lunch with Nick's Sicilian family including Cettina, the coolest nun I have ever met. Whew. So many! The people here are what make an already wonderful experience, simply amazing.

7. Sicilians really know how to celebrate. All summer long, every evening, there seems to be a reason to celebrate something. The harvest festival, the hunter's festival, music and dance performances, the Ferrari evening, *Ferragosto*

(the celebration of the Ascension of Mary). And then there are the evenings in which there is no specific *festa* organized, the Ciancianesi, like Italians all over the country, take part in the *passeggiata* or the evening stroll. It took me a little while to understand the *passeggiata*. In my North American mind, an evening stroll was about getting a little exercise, enjoying the surroundings, helping out my digestion. The first couple of times Nick and I went out for our evening stroll, when we had walked up and down the street once, I figured we were done. But this is not what the *passeggiata* is about. Sicilians go out for their evening stroll to visit. Who else is walking up and down the street or in the *piazza*? Who is sitting at the bar enjoying a *caffè*, *caffè* with brandy or *grappa*, wine or beer? Who is out walking with whom? I have learned to love walking up and down and the rare evenings when Nick and I don't go, I find I really miss this simple pleasure.

8. I asked Nick what he was most looking forward to and his unhesitating answer, not surprisingly, was 'going to the beach'. Many of the beaches on the west coast of Canada are covered in stones: stones worn smooth from the frigid waves on the beach, but stones nonetheless. They make interesting-looking beaches, but they are not so comfortable when it comes to stretching out and soaking up the sun. The Sicilian beaches, on the other hand, are, for the most part, covered in beautiful fine sand that stretches gradually down to the warm Mediterranean waters – perfect for swimming. There is very little more pleasurable than spending the day enjoying the Sicilian sun with your toes dug into warm sand as the salty sea-water evaporates from your tanned skin as you embrace your inner Italian and sport your skimpy bikini or speedo. Just a note on speedos

and bikinis: a trip to an Italian beach is a shock for many North Americans. Not all Italians are skinny models that have just stepped off the pages of Vogue. They are normal people with normal body sizes. Tall, thin, short, chubby – many are overweight however I would note that there are relatively few morbidly obese Italians compared to North America. What shocked me was how comfortable all these Italians appeared to be in their bathing suits. Skimpy bathing suits. Very skimpy bathing suits. Now, not all Italian women wear bikinis and not all Italian men wear Speedos, but you will rarely see someone covering themselves up with a robe or shirt after coming out of the water. Italians seem to revel in their bodies. I am certainly not an expert in the Italian psyche and so I will not hazard a guess at why this is, but the degree of body shame that many North Americans feel seems to be nonexistent on the Italian beaches. Experiencing this is liberating. It led to my daughter shedding her t-shirt and board shorts. It even eventually led to my shy husband buying and wearing the first Speedo of his life! As for me, I bought myself my first two-piece swimsuit since the time I was a toddler. Sitting on a beach in my two-piece suit anywhere in North America, what I would feel is likely shame, but sitting at Borgo Bonsignore, my favourite beach in Sicily, I am buoyed up by the comfort the Sicilians around me have in their own bodies. Now, every summer, I go to the beach in my new two-piece swimsuit and I revel in the sun and the sea and the joy in just being me.

"A man without a belly is like a sky without the stars."
Sicilian proverb

Maria Cacciato's Completely Easy and Delicious "S" Cookies

Ingredients:

6 Eggs at room temperature
1 lb. white sugar
1/2 lb. shortening melted
12 ounces milk, warmed
6 tsp. baking powder
2 ½ lbs. all purpose flour plus ¾ cup

Directions:

Preheat oven to 350F.
Heat shortening and milk until shortening is melted.
Beat eggs and mix into the shortening and milk.
Add sugar and mix thoroughly.
Add in baking powder and then flour, holding back the ¾ cup, and continue to mix thoroughly.
Spread the ¾ cup of flour on a work surface and take a heaping tablespoon of dough and roll it on the floured surface to make a "rope" about ¼ inch in diameter.
Cut each "rope" into 6-inch lengths.
Form S-shaped cookies and place on parchment paper on a cookie tray.
Bake until very lightly golden, approximately 13 minutes.

Makes approximately 150 cookies

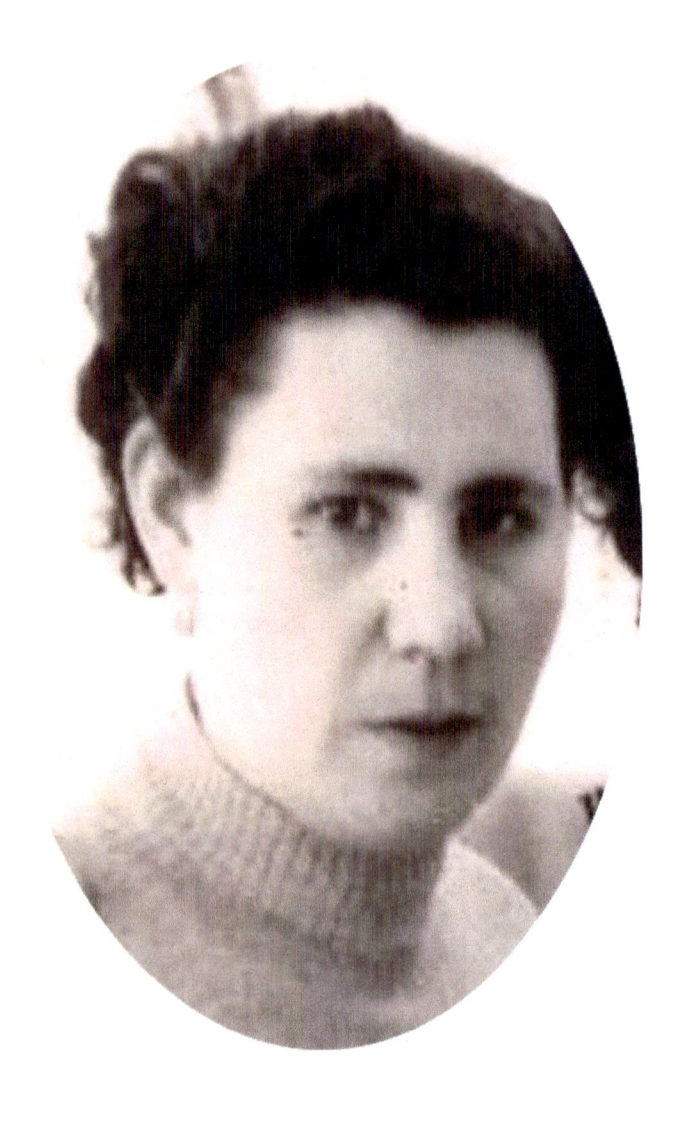

Chapter Nine
Top Ten Crazy Things About Sicily

I have never been much for using travel guides. Whenever I have travelled in the past, I have depended on advice from the people I met locally to find the restaurants, hotels, and the most interesting sites. Nick, on the other hand, would pack every book we owned on Italy if we had space and unlimited luggage weight. In 2012 on our first venture into Cianciana, I managed to keep him down to two books: *Top 10 Sicily* and the *Cadogan Guide to Sicily*.

While I haven't read a lot of travel guides, I am a reader. I usually have either a stack of real or virtual books sitting next to my bed waiting for me to read and this trip was no different with one exception – I didn't bring enough reading material. After the last of my books were finished, I found myself rummaging around in my husband's suitcase to see if there were any books that I didn't know about.

So, after finding no fiction (I prefer fiction over nonfiction and fantasy over everything else) I picked up Nick's *Cadogan Guide to Sicily* and *Top 10 Sicily* and started reading. The Cadogan guide was written by Dana Facaros and Michael Pauls. I haven't read (to my knowledge) anything else by these two but just from this guide I suspect they have a terrific sense of humour. As I read their guide, I kept coming across crazy things about Sicily that I had never heard before and as I did I would turn down the corner of the page so I could find them again and read them to Nick. We spent a pleasurable hour or so chuckling and guffawing over these (and other) anecdotes and tales. So, having compiled my list, here is my Top Ten Countdown of the crazy things I never knew about Sicily.

Number Ten

Sicily was under Byzantine rule in the 7th century ruled by Emperor Constans II. He was the first Emperor to travel to Sicily after the fall of Rome. He was seriously considering moving the Byzantine capital onto Sicilian territory at Siracusa when a courtier, furious over the slight to Constantinople, approached Constans II in the bath and killed him with a soap dish.

Number Nine

Arguably, one of history's most interesting mystic characters was Count Alessandro Cagliostro, born Guiseppe Balsamo in Palermo in 1743. He became adept at the use of pharmaceuticals and a master at forgery and through these talents scammed and conned his way into the highest of high society throughout Western Europe. His greatest coup as a con man involved convincing a goldsmith that he had discovered a cave on Monte Pellegrino that was full of treasure but guarded by devils that could only be lured away with 60 ounces of gold. The goldsmith brought the gold to the mountain but the "devils" (Cagliostro's accomplices) came out and beat the poor goldsmith until he ran away and they scarpered with the gold.

Number Eight

On the same theme of scam artists in Palermo, this story

happened much more recently. In 2005, a Palermitani couple bilked a poor woman out of 50,000 euros. How did they do this? They claimed to be vampires so convincingly that she truly believed that they would come and impregnate her with the Antichrist if she failed to pay up.

Number Seven

Lampedusa is a small, but stunningly beautiful island off the south coast of Sicily. It is about 20 square kilometres with a population of 4500. Its industries are fishing, agriculture and tourism. In 1987, Libya shot two scud missiles at Lampedusa. Fortunately for the Lampedusians, the aim of the Libyan military was not so great and the missiles fell into the sea. This was ostensibly in retaliation for the American bombings of Tripoli and Benghazi. Apparently the Libyans had a map in which the 51st US state was Lampedusa. (Just kidding).

Number Six

This one actually didn't come from my guidebooks but is one that I had seen on the television show "Urban Legends" and found later on the Internet. Starting in January 2004, in the tiny village of Canneto di Caronia, appliances in people's homes would burst into flame without warning. This moved from appliances to non-electrical things like mattresses and chairs. The fires became so frequent that the region's fire brigade set up permanent residence in Canneto di Caronia. People began to leave the town, rather than live under the constant threat of fire. Other residents believed that it was supernatural in origin and turned to the

Church to perform exorcisms. After a month, the fires began to diminish. And still, no one has any explanation. And to continue on the mystic theme...

Number Five

In Enna, in the absolute centre of Sicily (a.k.a. Umbilicus Sicilae or Sicily's navel), stands the Torre di Federico II. Other than being in the centre of Sicily, the spot has other significance. It is the crossroads of ancient Sicily's three main thoroughfares, which symbolize the Trinacria found on the Sicilian flag. The tower, however, is a mystery. Octagonal in shape, it has no known purpose. Federico II built the Castel del Monte in Puglia on the mainland, which is also octagonal in shape and also has no know purpose. In the 1960s, historian Umberto Massocco theorized that the spot was the centre of ley lines, similar to the ones found in England. On these lines can be found a variety of landmarks of historical and spiritual importance: Agrigento, Eraclea Minoa, Siracusa, and numerous others. His suggestion was that the whole island of Sicily is a large geometrical temple.

Number Four

Many people know the story of Archimedes running down the street yelling "Eureka", but if you don't, here it is. Archimedes, also known as the Wizard of Syracuse, was a mathematician and the cousin of Hieron II. Hieron had commissioned a golden crown to present to the gods at Delphi. Once the crown was finished, he asked Archimedes to find a way to ensure that the goldsmith had not cheated him and used a cheaper metal on the inside. While sitting in the bathtub in his home in Syracuse, Archimedes came up with the idea of using displacement to prove if the crown was solid gold or not. So excited by his discovery, he jumped out of his bath and ran naked down the streets of Syracuse shouting "Eureka".

Number Three

Sicilian history seems to be full of magicians and wizards. Somerset Maugham wrote a story called "The Magician" which was based on the true-to-life story of Aleister Crowley, originally from Leamington, England. Crowley was referred to as the Magician of Cefalù. Cefalù is a tourist town with a stunning bay and a white glowing beach. To see this town, one would never guess that it had hosted a cult centred on drugs, sex and black magic. Crowley established the Abbey of Thelema to hold "rites" that would, he said, be the successor to Christianity. Crowley referred to himself as "The Beast" and encouraged people to do whatever they pleased, no matter how perverse. He was famous for his pornographic murals and his book "Diary of a Drug Addict". Eventually he was thrown out of Italy by Mussolini. In 1947, on his death, his will requested that he be buried in the town of Cefalù. The town of Cefalù denied his request. (I wonder why?)

Number Two

The little village of Villalba is at first glance an ordinary Sicilian village – no particular reason to visit this village over any other except for this. Near the village is Pizzo di Lauro, a mountain peak. Rumour has it that the greatest treasure in

all the world is hidden on this peak. According to Facaros
and Pauls, this treasure is said to be guarded by fairies
living in a palace. People trying to find the treasure
disappear on the mountain and all that can be found of them
is their groans, moaning the following: "Pizzo di Lauro, for
your riches we have lost our lives and our salvation."

Number One

And finally, my favourite crazy story about Sicily is. . . In
1064, the Normans made their first attempt to attack and
seize Palermo. Sadly, they bivouacked up a hill covered
with a particular species of tarantula whose bites caused the
soldiers to suffer from a very unpleasant attack of painful
farts, thus ending their first attack on Palermo. No one could
make this stuff up. Seriously.

"Hunger is a hooker and a thief"
Sicilian proverb

Cazzilli (Fried Potato Pancakes)

When translating the name of this very yummy street
food, I gave the "G-rated" translation. I have been assured,
however, that *cazzilli* actually translates into, well, "small
dick". My guess is that a woman named these tasty treats
as I cannot imagine any red-blooded Sicilian man even
making an indirect reference to the possibility of the
existence of a "tiny member". Interestingly, in Italian there
are a number of different kinds of foods named after parts of

the human anatomy or vice versa. There are some Italian cookies called *Ossi dei Morti* or Bones of the Dead and Sicilian pastries call *minni di virgini* or breasts of the virgins. *Orecchiette*, a kind of pasta, means "little ears". *Fica*, which literally means fig, is a somewhat rude euphemism for vagina and the expression "*porco mondo*", literally "pig world", is used to mean "damn it all".

Ingredients:

6 medium russet potatoes
3 large eggs
½ cup of pecorino, parmesan, or caciocavallo cheese depending on your preference
1 ¼ cups of fine Italian bread crumbs
2 minced garlic cloves
2 tbsp. chopped parsley, oregano, or basil depending on your preference plus 1 tbsp. chopped mint
salt and pepper
vegetable oil for frying

Directions:

Boil unpeeled potatoes until they are cooked through.
Drain and allow to cool, then place in the refrigerator until they are completely chilled.
Peel chilled potatoes.
Mash or rice potatoes ensuring that there are no lumps left and they are completely smooth.
Separate the eggs and mix 2/3 of the yoke into the potatoes.
Stir garlic, herbs and salt and pepper into the potato and egg mixture.
Add the cheese and ¼ cup of breadcrumbs and mix well.
Roll the potato mixture into a tube-shape about 3" long. Set aside.
Beat the egg whites until frothy. Fold in the remaining egg yoke.
Place the remaining bread crumbs into a shallow bowl.
Dip the potato tubes into the egg mixture followed by the breadcrumbs.
Place on a sheet of wax paper on a plate and then into the freezer for 30 minutes – this will help them hold their shape while they are frying.
After 30 minutes, pour vegetable oil into a medium saucepan and heat to a high (not smoking) temperature.
Remove the potato tubes from the freezer.
Fry a few of the potato tubes at a time until they are golden brown.
Remove from the oil with a slotted spoon and lay on a paper towel-lined plate. Serve hot.

Serves 6.

Chapter Ten
Salt: The Seasoning of Life

Recently, Nick and I visited one of my favourite towns on the west coast of Sicily. Trapani has the smallest international airport to be found on the island but it is well worth the Ryan Air flight. It is small enough that there is quite literally no customs or immigration when you land. You simply pick up your suitcases and walk out of the airport.

Another thing about Trapani that I love are the salt flats. Some of the best sea salt in the world comes from the fields outside of Trapani. You might ask why salt would be so interesting to me, but then, in my other life I taught history and in history, salt has had the king's role.

Salt and the development of human communities have gone hand in hand. Salt exists in places where sea water has evaporated forming outcroppings of salt (salt licks), shallow caverns that need to be mined or salt beds along the sea. Animals would find their way to the natural salt licks creating paths, which later turned to roads and communities plopped themselves down along the way. As hunters, humans had enough salt in their diet from the meat they consumed, but once gathering became the way we subsisted, salt became necessary for life. Most available salt lay underground, making it difficult to access. Thus, as any first year economics student could tell you, the law of supply and demand kicked into high gear and, because of its scarcity, became quite literally worth its weight in gold. Trade in salt boomed.

Trade routes developed crisscrossing northern Africa,

the Mediterranean, and going as far east as China, becoming intrinsically intertwined with the spice trade. In fact, Venice's importance and wealth was built by carrying salt to Constantinople and trading it for Eastern spices. Salt became currency in many places in Africa. Abyssinia used slabs of rock salt about 10" long and 2" thick called *amôlés*. Greeks and Romans bought slaves with salt and Roman soldiers' pay consisted partly of salt and was called *solarium argentum* from which the present day word "salary" comes. Salt had the power to strengthen or dissolve governments. Taxes collected on salt could fill a king's coffers making him and his country wealthy. Conversely, these taxes could be the downfall of a king or government. In France, the taxes on salt were so outrageously high that it helped start the French Revolution and led to the beheading of Louis XVI and Marie Antoinette. In India, Mahatma Gandhi took his followers to the sea to make their own salt, protesting the high salt taxes imposed by the British government, leading the Indian people one step closer to emancipation.

Over time, salt has become the centre in many expressions and superstitions. Salt can be used as an antiseptic, which led to the belief that salt could purify us of bad luck or evil spirits. In Japan, even today, sumo wrestlers toss salt into the ring before beginning to wrestle as a way of purifying their space. Spilling salt is considered unlucky and must be followed by tossing a little salt over the left shoulder, which was considered 'sinister' and had to be purified. Leonardo da Vinci painted an overturned saltcellar in front of Judas in The Last Supper indicating the evil he was about to cause.

Salt is thought to bring prosperity, which is why many people make a gift of salt to newlyweds, those who have purchased a new house and when visiting people on New Years. Salt could protect against witchcraft, curses and the 'evil eye' or *mal'occhio* in Italian.

English is full of expressions using salt as a metaphor or simply referring to past human experience with salt. 'Go back to the salt mines' referred to the backbreaking work that slaves did bringing salt to the surface from underground. You can still frequently hear things like 'It went through him like a dose of salts' referring to past medicinal uses of salt or 'She is worth her salt' harking back to the days in which salt was used as currency. A very apt Sicilian proverb tells us that to recognize a real friend, you have to together have eaten three bushels of salt. Other Italians say '*Avere sale in zucca*' or 'you have salt on your pumpkin' meaning to be very clever. To an Italian, you're clever if you know to sprinkle salt on pumpkin and other winter squashes to balance their natural sweetness.

"The satiated don't believe the hungry."
Sicilian Proverb

Caponata (Eggplant Antipasto)

Do you love eggplant? I know I do. Eggplant has the ability to pair up nicely with whatever else you might be cooking. *Caponata* is a very yummy and easy to make antipasto.

Ingredients:

3 eggplants
3 bell peppers – green, yellow and red
½ pound of green pitted olives
1 yellow or white onion
1 ¾ oz. of sultana raisins
1 ¾ oz. of pine nuts
1 celery stock
1 ½ tsp. tomato paste
2 tbsp. salted capers
5 ¼ fluid oz. vinegar
1 tbsp. sugar
1 sprig of basil
Extra virgin olive oil
Salt and pepper
3 tbsp. crushed peanuts

Directions:

Wash the eggplants and peppers then dice after removing

seeds. Put the eggplant in a colander, sprinkle with salt and leave to stand for about half an hour then rinse and dry.

In a large frying pan heat plenty of oil and fry the eggplant. When golden brown lift them with a slotted spoon and lay out on paper towel to absorb any remaining oil.

In the same oil fry peppers, then lift out with a slotted spoon and keep aside.

In the same pan, sauté the finely chopped onion (if necessary add a little extra oil)

Add the celery, washed and drained capers, raisins, pine nuts, pitted olives, and sauté with care.

As soon as the ingredients brown, add the tomato paste dissolved in a little warm water as well as the chopped basil. Season with salt and pepper to taste and simmer for a few minutes.

Add the vinegar into which you have dissolved the sugar, and then add the eggplant and peppers and stir gently.

After a couple of minutes turn off the heat and transfer the caponata into a serving dish and allow to cool then sprinkle with peanuts before serving.

Serves 4.

Chapter Eleven
One Saturday Evening in Cianciana

In the evening, like most people in most Sicilian towns, we do our *passeggiata* or walkabout. Every evening there are hundreds of people out, however one night during our second Sicilian summer, it seemed that more than half the town was collected in the *piazza*. Young girls dressed in their very best – stiletto heels balancing on cobblestones, hair and make-up perfect; they looked very much as if they were attending a film or art gallery opening rather than the requisite evening stroll in this small Sicilian village. Young men, hair precisely quaffed into a faux-hawk or shaved on the sides with a ducktail on top, crisp and clean polo shirts with the collars turned up. They eyed the girls who pretended they didn't see them but giggled anyways. Old men sat on the benches outside the social club, discussing the problems of the world – young people, politics, employment – finding solutions that only they will hear. Visitors – expats and ex-*Ciancianesi* alike, wandered and admired the buildings, and discussed in a myriad of languages what a terrific place this is. Everywhere on the street, you could see husbands and wives walking arm in arm. This is probably an influence of the large expat community – it is most definitely not a regular occurrence amongst the older Sicilians in other towns.

Once we reached the centre of Cianciana we could see why so many people were out and about. The Ferrari club from Ribera had come to Cianciana. The roads had been blocked off to regular traffic and the drivers were giving children rides up and down the town, engines roaring and tires spinning.

Later, they parked their Ferraris, cherry red, on Corso Vittorio Emmanuel outside one of the larger bars in Cianciana called, ironically, The Canadian. The *Ciancianesi* (and the expats as well) flocked around these machines and took pictures. Nick and I were not immune to the excitement and we took our pictures with these powerful cars as well.

On an island with an unemployment rate at 25%, I wondered how so many people in such a small town could afford a Ferrari. Unsure, I guessed that the answer might lie in the ancient houses. Very few of these houses have mortgages. They have been passed from grandparents to parents to children. With no rent or mortgage to pay, it is perhaps easier to live if one is under employed or unemployed. This is simply conjecture on my part. I really don't know the answer.

We wandered back in the direction of our favourite bar, Bar Antico Trieste. One of our newly-made friends, Gaetano, stopped us. Are we going to stay for the music? It is supposed to start at 9:30 – in 15 minutes. There will be a live band and dancing. Sit, sit! Have a *caffè*! We joined Gaetano at one of the tables set out on the street. He bought us each *il caffè*, an espresso, and we sat and chatted about Cianciana in the summer. Gaetano was born here. Then, as now he lived alone – no wife or children, but his sister who lived down the street, would frequently stop in to check on him. He told us about the clock tower – built in 1908 – and how life here had changed over the years. He told us how in the summer, people would stay out until two or three in the morning and the bars don't close until 4am. We chatted for nearly two hours but there was no music.

The instruments were set up and from time to time someone – presumably musicians – came to fiddle with the set up but no music played. Finally, we took our leave of Gaetano.

My eyelids were growing heavy. I obviously didn't have the stamina of the *Ciancianesi*. As we walked home, I could hear thunder roll and see lightening flash off in the distance. Once in the house, we sat at the kitchen table to drink a glass of water before we went to bed. In the distance we could hear the music start. A rock version of "*Volare*". Later in the night I woke, cold for the first time since we arrived here. It was raining – hard. The water drummed on the terracotta tiles outside our window. I listened to the sound until it soothed me back to sleep.

"Eat warm and drink cold."
Sicilian Proverb

Pasta a "Picchu Pacchiu (Spaghetti with Fresh Tomatoes and Garlic)

Ingredients:

1 kg. of very ripe red tomatoes
4 cloves of garlic
1 tbsp. chili seeds
6 leaves of fresh basil
1 ½ cups extra virgin olive oil
1 lb. of spaghetti
¼ cup grated caciocavallo or parmesan cheese

Directions:

Blanche the tomatoes, peel and remove seeds chop into small chunks and set aside in a large bowl.
Sliver the garlic and chop the basil and add to tomato chunks.
Add chili seeds and olive oil into the tomatoes and stir all together.
Cover the bowl and set aside for approximately 3 hours.
Cook spaghetti according to the instructions, drain and then set in a bowl.
Add the marinated tomatoes, stir into the pasta and sprinkle with either grated caciocavallo or parmesan cheese.

Serves 4.

Chapter Twelve
Cappuccino in the Afternoon? Must be a Foreigner

Coffee marks time in Italy. *Espresso* at the bar on the way to work in the morning. *Cappuccino* before noon. Gulp back your *espresso* and head out of the bar in minutes. It is a caffeine-laced labyrinth if you want to immerse yourself in coffee culture in Italy. Here are a few rules that I gleaned from the *Telegraph* article "Italian Coffee Culture: A Guide", Sept. 30, 2009.

Let's start with the word '*espresso*'. In North America, and I presume in the UK, *espresso* is used in coffee shops or when you purchase coffee in the store to indicate a particular kind of coffee. In Italy, all coffee is *espresso* therefore if you simply want an *espresso* you order *il caffè*. I remember making this mistake several years ago. We were in a hotel in Marina di Ravenna that included breakfast. The first morning our hostess asked us if we wanted *il caffè* and I specified *espresso*. She gave me a very odd look and said, "*Sì, il caffè.*" then shook her head presumably thinking she was dealing with an ignorant foreigner – which I was – at least about coffee.

Coffee is ordered in a bar. Bars are not quite the same as in North America. Besides serving alcohol, they also serve coffee, soft drinks, *gelato*, pastry, *panini*, pizza, and (if you are lucky and in Sicily) *arancini*. Children can enter bars. Bars open in the morning and, at least in Cianciana in the summer, stay open until 2 or 3 in the morning. Sometimes even later.

In Canada, if I go to a coffee shop and order a coffee, I will sit and sip my coffee taking my time to finish it. In Italy, if you drop by a bar to order *il caffè*, you stand at the bar, stir in heaping spoonfuls of sugar and toss your coffee back quickly. Afterwards you drink the glass of water they often offer you, and then you head off out the door – no wasted time.

What do you call your coffee? Here are a few of the options you can order in a bar.

Il caffè – we would call this *espresso*. It will have a thin, light brown foam on top, which is called '*crema*'. You will hear the gentlemen in the bar discussing the quality of the *crema* as it is considered a very important part of the quality of the coffee.

Caffè Hag – this is decaf. It is the name of the largest producer of decaf coffee and has been adopted as the general name.

Caffè Americano – this is a much weaker and more bitter coffee and is closer to what is normally served in North America. Italians also call this *acqua sporca* or "dirty water", which tells you what they think of it.

Caffè con Panna – *espresso* topped with whipped cream. Yum!

Caffè Corretto – *espresso* with a small shot of liquor – often *grappa* (very strong Italian liqueur) but other liqueurs can be used.

Cappuccino – pretty much the same as North America.

Caffè Macchiato – *espresso* with just a touch of milk and foam.

Caffè Freddo - strictly speaking, this is just cold *espresso,* however it can range from a pre-sweetened cold *espresso* with milk that they store in the fridge to something much grander - freshly made *espresso,* shaken with ice and sweetened as you like with a perfect *crema* on top. If you are in Cianciana, Dario in the bar closest the *Chiesa Madre* (mother church) is the master.

Just a note on ordering coffee in Italy – Italians, and not just Sicilians, NEVER order coffee with milk after 12 noon. It is considered very bad for you to drink warm milk, even in coffee, in the afternoon or later. Only foreigners will order a *cappuccino* or *macchiato* after the morning has come to a close. I don't know for certain where this belief came from. It is pure speculation on my part, but I wonder if it harkens back to the pre-refrigeration days in which milk came fresh from the cow or goat in the morning, but might be soured by the heat of the afternoon. Your guess is as good as mine.

Federica from Bar Giancarlo in Trapani makes the best cappuccino!

> "A trusted friend is a priceless treasure."
> **Sicilian Proverb**

Gina and Enza's Easy Coffee *Granita*

Granita is a delicious, non-dairy alternative to *gelato*. This recipe came to me from our neighbours just up the hill.

Ingredients:

2 ¼ cups of water
1 ¾ cups of sugar
1 cup espresso

Directions:

Bring water to a boil.
Gradually stir in the sugar, stirring continually until all the sugar is dissolved.
Add the *espresso* and stir.
Remove from heat and let cool.
When cool enough, pour into a plastic container and place in the freezer.
As the *granita* starts to freeze, remove from the freezer and stir briefly.
Continue to stir every 30 minutes or so until it is completely frozen.
To serve, using a heavy metal spoon, scrape ice crystals from the frozen *granita* until you have a bowlful.
To create lemon or green tea flavoured granita, replace the *espresso* with either lemon juice or green tea. For a juice flavoured *granita*, replace the *espresso* with juice and reduce

the sugar slightly to taste, depending on the sweetness of the juice.

Serves 6.

Chapter Thirteen
Coffee Culture and Italian Names

The last chapter was about coffee but as it is such an important part of Sicilian culture, I thought coffee was worth at least a second chapter.

In Sicily, Nick and I take part in the evening unofficial

entertainment – *passeggiata*. *Passeggiata*, or evening stroll is all about to "see-and-be-seen". It is the cultural philosophy of *bella figura* in a visible form. What is *bella figura*? Strictly speaking, it means to cut a beautiful figure but truly it is much more than that. My best experiences in Italy and Sicily have been when people show kindness for no other reason than kindness' sake. That's the true *bella figura*. Both can be seen during *passeggiata*. People are dressed to the nines. It is the premier social event of the day. In Cianciana *passeggiata* takes place after dinner, starting at about 9:30 and continuing sometimes as late as 2 or 3am. Most of the town turns up in their best and most fashionable clothes; hair and make-up perfectly done and with the most up-to-date smartphone gripped in their manicured hands.

Each town has its own main street *piazza f*or strolling – in Cianciana it is Corso Vittorio Emanuele.

"Passeggiata is a babble of lively conversation as everyone window shops their way up and down the street, everyone checking out everyone else (and even more crucially, being checked out), bumping into friends and acquaintances…" Reid's Italy

For tourists it is unlikely that they would happen across someone they know as they wander, but for those of us who have set down roots in a particular place, it is impossible to do *passeggiata* without bumping into a friendly face and being invited to stop at the bar for a coffee – an active example of *bella figura*.

One night found us making our way down Corso Vittorio Emanuele (Every town has a street called Corso Vittorio

Emanuele – Vittorio Emanuele II was the first king of the unified Italy). As we wandered, we bumped into Gaetano-the-stone-mason. Gaetano-the-stone-mason was the first Ciancianese we met other than the people from MyHouse who helped us buy our home. Gaetano-the-stone-mason is a mostly retired gentleman – and I do mean gentleman in the very best sense of the word – who seems to collect acquaintances with the foreign community. Gaetano-the-stone-mason insisted we stop for *il caffè* and a *gelato* at the Trieste Bar. While we were sitting there, he struck up a conversation with a brother and sister who were visiting from Belgium which lead to a tête-à-tête between the five of us that took place in four languages – French, Italian, Sicilian and English. This is one of the magical things about Cianciana and about *passeggiata* – language and cultural barriers seem to drop in the face of both the friendly nature of the *Ciancianesi* and the mutual love of caffeine.

After we said "*Buona sera*" to Gaetano-the-stone-mason and our new *Belgique* acquaintances, we slowly wandered down the road, around the corner at the *Chiesa Madre* (mother church) until we got to the Canadian Pizza Bar. Gaetano-the-barkeep (he owns Canadian Pizza with his Sicilian-Canadian wife) called out "Hey, Canadians! Come over here!" He poured both Nick and himself shots from some rather wicked looking bottle and tossed it back. Not to be outdone, Nick followed suit and handed back the shot glass with a nod and a comment, "Nice." We decided to sit for a bit and watch the stream of people. With Gaetano-the-barkeep, I knew I could make the terrible faux-pas of ordering a *cappuccino* in the evening. Nick ordered *il caffè* and a croissant. Gaetano-the-barkeep brought us our order with a laugh and the comment – "You crazy Canadians, ordering breakfast at night!" We sat there and said "*Ciao*" and "*Buona sera!*" to everyone we knew who went by, including Tony-the-bulldog-owner, who always loves to stop and practice his English with us.

When we left Canadian Pizza, we made our way back down the main street where we were stopped by Tony-the-Marxist. Our relationship with Tony-the-Marxist is a perfect example of how I know just enough Italian to get myself into trouble, but not enough to get out of trouble. One summer at *Ferragosto* – the biggest of the summer festivals – we were introduced to Tony-the-Marxist for the first time. Nick asked him why he wasn't in church at mass along with most of the town. Tony-the-Marxist made a dismissive hand gesture and said, "*Sono socialisto*". In other words, as a socialist, he has nothing to do with religion. Now, in Italy, a socialist is much more closely aligned to communism and Marxist thinking whereas in Canada, a socialist is really more likely just a follower of the New Democrat Party, which describes both Nick and me. So, without thinking, I pipe up with, "*Noi siamo anche socialisti!*" "We are socialists too!" I immediately realized my mistake but, as I said, my Italian was not good enough to extricate myself. Well, from that point on we were Tony-the-Marxist's best foreign friends and now whenever we see him downtown, he insists we stop for coffee. So, bumping into Tony-the-Marxist that night meant our third coffee of the evening and a discussion of our trip to Sardinia. We sat at the Bar San Antonio and were served by – of course – Gaetano, the owner. After our third coffee for the evening (and fifth coffee for the day), we nipped up a side street to head home, knowing that even one more coffee would have us up even beyond the 1am sleep-time that we knew was certainly in front of us. Now, you may wonder, why is it that we are always the invitees and not the inviters? Well, in Cianciana they say the guest never pays. The day that we will be allowed to buy coffee for our friends, we will know that we have finally become adopted as full members of this community. Until then, in spite of trying unsuccessfully to reciprocate, we will be the grateful recipients of the very generous nature of the *Ciancianesi*.

On a side note about Italian names, you could be forgiven for thinking, after reading the start of this chapter, that every man in Cianciana was called either Gaetano or Tony (Antonio). That is not the case. Our neighbours to the right are Guiseppe, Anna and their son is… oh, Antonio. Down the street are our other neighbours, um… Anna and Guiseppe. Their daughter, Franca, has been a wonderful friend to us. In fact, before we went downtown that particular evening, we sat out on the street talking with Anna and Guiseppe and Antonio, Anna and Guiseppe, Franca and her sons… Antonio and Gaetano. Wait, I am not really clearing this up am I? There was the car dealer employee, a very helpful man who drove us to Sciacca to get insurance. His name was… oh, um, Gaetano. Then there is Gaetano who works for Scott, the contractor who did the renovations on our house. I am being a bit tongue in cheek here; we have Sicilian friends and acquaintances of all different names: Fabrizio, Silvestro, Enzo, Silvio, Onofrio, Calgero, Alfonso, Carmelo, Vincenzo, Gianfranco, Massimo, Marta, Francesca, Enza, Gina, Maria, Giulia … The repetition of names comes from a couple of practices in Italian culture. Eldest sons are named usually after the paternal grandfather and the eldest daughters after the paternal grandmother. Nick is named after his grandfather,

Nicola and so he has at least four cousins also named Nicola. Nick's sister is Tina and his cousin is Cettina, both of whom are named after their grandmother, Concettina. There is also a practice of naming children after the patron saint of the town. In Cianciana, the patron saint is San Antonio – thus all the Tonys. In Capizzi, where Nick's family originates, the patron saint is San Giacomo. Nick's Uncle Jack (Giacomo) and cousin Jackie (Giacomina) are both named for him. Meeting Nick's family for the first time was like the scene from My Big Fat Greek Wedding in which the fiance's parents meet the Greek family for the first time. "This is my brother and his children Diane, Angelo and Nick. This is my other brother and his children Diane, Angelo and Nick. This is my sister and her children Diane, Angelo and Nikki…" At least, if I forgot someone's name, I could probably guess it in two or three tries!

Waiting for coffee with Tony.

> "The devil eats macaroni with the monk and drinks wine with the politician."
> Sicilian Proverb

Franca Tamburello's Amazing Potato Pizza

In Cianciana, Franca makes, of course, her own pizza dough. In recognition of how busy our lives often are, I am calling for a premade pizza shell in this recipe.

Ingredients:

2 pizza shells
1 cup extra virgin olive oil
15 new potatoes
2 onions
2 cloves of garlic
¼ cup grated parmesan cheese
2 tsp. dried oregano
freshly ground pepper

Directions:

Preheat oven to 400F.
Wash the new potatoes and thinly slice.
Dice onions and crush garlic.
Combine onions, garlic, oregano, salt, pepper and parmesan cheese and olive oil. Mix well.
Add potatoes to the mixture and turn over and over until all the potatoes have been covered with the mixture then leave

to marinate.

Spread the potato mixture on the pizza shell and bake pizzas until the potatoes have taken on a golden colour and a crispy texture.

Remove, slice and eat hot.

This makes 2 pizzas.

Chapter Fourteen
Going Gluten Free in Italy

When I was diagnosed with moderate to severe arthritis, I did some research on things that might help ease my inflammation. Much to my chagrin and deep disappointment, I discovered that gluten can add to inflammation. I cut gluten out of my diet and sure enough, my pain began to lessen.

Shortly after cutting out gluten I took a group of teenagers on a tour of Paris. This was a wonderful trip overall but a nightmare as far as food went. It started on the plane. I won't name the airline – suffice it to say it was a major carrier. Now, airline food is notoriously bad. I feel like I can make this statement fairly because it was a topic of much discussion in my family. My Uncle Pat had worked for the now defunct Canadian Airlines as the coordinator for all food on all flights originating at YVR – or Vancouver International Airport to those of you uninitiated into airport abbreviations. I do not believe that the inedibility of the food on Canadian Airlines had much to do with Uncle Pat but I may have been the only one in the family that thought so. My family didn't fly that often (other than Uncle Pat and my aunt), but when any of us did, the first question when the family member returned was, "How was the food?" This was followed by a blow-by-blow description of the lack of taste, the terrible texture, and how it was too hot/cold/much/little, and so on. Really, my poor Uncle Pat was doomed from the start. I have a hard time believing that my jolly, kind uncle would purposely supply disgusting food to the Canadian Airline travellers, but to my childish ears, that's what it sounded like. But I digress.

As I said, my food troubles started on the plane. I had contacted the tour company and requested gluten-free meals. This is what I got. The main course was made up primarily of quinoa. I have two problems with quinoa. To start with, quinoa is a staple food of many Indigenous people in South America. When we, the privileged of the Global North discovered that there was a "magically healthy" grain from the Global South, we began buying it up in huge quantities. Of course, increased demand means decreased supply, which means increased price. The people who most need the quinoa have been priced out of the market. That's my first problem. My second problem? Well, to my probably un-quinoa-sophisticated palate, quinoa tastes like cardboard. There, I've said it. Go ahead and send me angry emails if you like – it won't help me find quinoa any more delicious. So, there I was, faced with a dish of quinoa with a few soybeans and corn kernels thrown in. The other end of the dish was watery chicken. I don't mean that there was water in the dish around the chicken, although that would have been disgusting enough. No, what I mean was that when I pressed the chicken with my fork, water came out. It was, for all intents and purposes, a chicken sponge. Mmmmmm. Yummy. Then, there was a small dish – I expect that this was what passed for a salad. They had taken all of the leftover soybeans and corn, thrown in a little shredded carrot and a whole bunch of salad dressing. And then there was what must have been someone's idea of a joke. A brownie and a white bun. Not marked gluten-free anywhere. So, do I roll the dice and hope that I won't be in pain for the next ten days? I decided not to risk it. Fortunately, I have travelled enough to know to carry my own snacks with me. It was a damn good thing I did because, after what was pretty much an inedible dinner (other than the salad), we were served breakfast the next morning. Scrambled eggs swimming in some kind of sauce with little potato cubes. On the side was…. wait for it…. a white bun. Oh, did I mention I can't eat eggs? Well, actually, it's egg whites and I haven't been able to eat them for, well, basically my whole life. They make me sick as dog. Even the smell of scrambled eggs is enough to turn my stomach to the point that I have no desire to eat. Imagine being the person who is nauseated by the smell of scrambled eggs and all around in this enclosed space is... scrambled eggs. Lovely.

For the gluten-free, Paris is challenging. In the land of croissants and French bread, NOBODY understood what gluten was. In one restaurant, the dinner for the tour group was pizza. My poor tour guide was tearing his hair out. My French is terrible – enough to understand some of what was being said but definitely not enough to help him explain about gluten. When he explained to the staff in the restaurant that I had to eat gluten-free, I thought he was going to cry when they offered to make me spaghetti.

Fast forward to Italy. Before I started going to Italy, I assumed that everything was pasta or pizza. Or Caesar salad. I think most people from North America might be forgiven for that assumption, considering that most North American Italian restaurants focus on those three food groups. But, after spending time in Sicily I realized that:

1. Caesar salad isn't really Italian, and
2. assuming that Italians only eat pasta and pizza is the same as assuming Canadians only eat burgers. Or poutine. Or maple syrup.

To my absolute delight, I discovered Sicilians really understand about gluten. Andrew Curry of The New York Times, wrote an article on June 26, 2014, talking about his experience travelling with his very gluten-free wife. When I read his article I was surprised to learn that the Italians had figured out that there were issues with gluten long before it was discussed in North America or in other parts of Europe. The *Associazione Italiana Celiachia*, or AiC, established in 1979, estimates the number of people who suffer from celiac disease in Italy is likely above half a million, and that does not include people like me who are simply gluten sensitive. In a country in which eating is such an important part of life and culture, not being able to partake in the very social activity of cooking and eating is taken very seriously, to the point that people with celiac disease can buy gluten-free products in the *farmacia* (pharmacy) and are given an allowance from the national health system in order to cover the extra costs.

It is not unusual to find a pizzeria that offers gluten-free crusts. Even out in the remote wilds of Sicily, people with gluten issues can find what they need. When we were visiting our good friends Linda and Bruno in their home high up in the hills above Noto and Avola, we sent Nick and Bruno off for take-out pizza. They came riding home on Bruno's scooter, Nick clutching a pile of pizza boxes as Bruno careened wildly around the corners of the terrifyingly windy road up the cliffs to their home. After Nick had caught his breath, he was excited to say he had found a gluten-free pizza for me. Even on Vancouver Island, where the awareness around food sensitivities is fairly high, not every Italian restaurant or pizzeria carries gluten-free products. We were both surprised and delighted at the availability of choices that were *senza glutine*!

> **"On St. Francis' Day [October 4th] sow parsley".**
> **Sicilian proverb.**

Mint-flavoured beans

Every year in Cianciana on July 31st, there is a harvest festival. Nick and I have been volunteering for three years now. Generally we are pouring the wine or the water, but others are scooping out steaming plates of delicious fava beans. Beans are a staple in the Sicilian diet. This particular recipe actually calls for the big white Spanish beans. The first time I tried it out, I was in Canada and had trouble finding Spanish beans. Instead, I tried using chickpeas. It was a resounding success.

Ingredients:

1 large can of chickpeas
1 stock of celery chopped
3 garlic cloves sliced
4 cups water
2 tbsp. dried mint
1 tbsp. parsley
¼ cup white vinegar
¼ cup olive oil

Directions:

Put the chopped celery, garlic, dried mint and water into a saucepan.
Bring to a boil and then simmer for 3 – 4 minutes.

Drain chickpeas and put into a non-plastic bowl with a lid.
Strain the celery, garlic and mint out of the boiled water.
Pour the boiled water over the bean mixture.
Cover the bowl and put in the refrigerator for about an hour.
Drain the chickpeas, pour olive oil and vinegar over the
beans and mix.

Serves 4.

Chapter Fifteen
Telecom Italia and Amazon Duke It Out

The birth of this book was actually a blog. Originally, the intension was to just keep a record for friends and family of our great adventure into the world of Sicilian home ownership. The blog, "My Sicilian Home", grew into much more and Nick and I met many people who stopped us on the street and said, "Hey, aren't you the ones from that blog?" Some of my very best friends in Sicily came from that kind of meeting and so the blog has become an integral part of our lives in Cianciana and in other parts of Sicily.

There are a few things that are absolutely indispensible when writing a blog. Firstly, you must have an idea. It doesn't have to be a unique idea – this post is an example of that – it doesn't even have to be a very good / funny / pithy idea, although those do make better blog posts. One thing that is absolutely indispensible is good Internet access. You can write the funniest, brightest, wittiest, pithiest post ever composed in the course of history on this planet but if you don't have Internet access no one will ever know what a truly amazing writer you are! (tongue slightly in cheek here).

My experiences in Sicily have given me so many ideas for posts. So why am I not posting every day then? Well, let me tell you.

Our first year in Cianciana, the year we bought our house, we had no Internet access of our own. Mornings could find us huddled over our electronic devices in the MyHouse Real Estate office where we had access to their Wi-Fi.

Later, when we were in Agira staying in the ultra rustic stone "cottage" built by Nick's great-grandfather we, of course, had no Wi-Fi whatsoever. I thought I would lose my mind. Nick, my wonderful husband, is an introvert by nature. He is quite happy staying home and playing solitaire on his iPad. Me, not so much. I am an extrovert and need to recharge by being around other people. So, staying for several days out in the middle of nowhere with my somewhat less than garrulous husband and no Wi-Fi, albeit in what was actually a rather beautiful setting, I was pretty much ready to be carted off to Bedlam.

Needless to say, the following year I told Nick in no uncertain terms that we HAD to get Internet. As it was our first year in Cianciana and we didn't know very many people yet, we went to the one person we did know who had, to that point, been able to answer all kinds of questions for us. Gianfranco, our neighbour down the road and the owner of Tutti Regalo, a gift / kitchenware / beach supply /stationary / etc. etc. store, suggested we try the WIND *chiave* (WIND Internet key). If you don't know what an Internet key is, it's a little device that looks like a USB memory stick that you plug into your laptop or whatever, punch in a password and bingo bango, you are on the Internet. Or at least that's the plan. With our WIND Internet key we would click on Safari or Chrome or Firefox and then (cue the Jeopardy music) we would wait. And wait. And wait. And then we would… wait some more. We discovered if we were not online before 7am or after 10pm, there was not much point in even playing with the thing. We battled the whole summer with the WIND Internet key. We also discovered later that the problem was that the WIND cell towers were behind the mountains across the way from us meaning that frequently the reception was non-existent.

Needless to say, the following year I told Nick in no uncertain terms that we HAD to get DIFFERENT Internet. That year we went to Massimo. Massimo had been tremendously helpful the year before. He had installed our antenna so we could watch 150 channels of bad American reality TV dubbed into Italian. At least if you are watching Say Yes To The Dress or Duck Dynasty you can guess what is going on as opposed to the shopping network(s) –

yes, there are numerous Italian shopping networks selling items that I had not a hope of figuring out – or old cheesy, badly acted Italian films. He had also saved us from ruining our washing machine on its first use because he noticed right away that the reno guy had installed in incorrectly and it was about to implode. So we had, and still have, lots of reasons for trusting Massimo. His suggestion was for us to use a Tre (3) Italia little modem device that worked off the Tre Italia cellphone towers visible above our mountains so presumably no reception problems. We could get Internet all summer for just €20! Sounded like a good plan to us. We bought the device and €20 worth of time and took it home to use it. It was great! It worked consistently at anytime of the day or night. It worked, that is, for about 3 days when it asked for us to buy more time. We did. And then we did again. When we had spent €150 in less than 6 weeks we went back to Massimo and said "What the hell! Excuse me Massimo, this seems to be taking more than the €20 you suggested it would." Actually, this wasn't our first visit back to Massimo. He spends most of his time out installing various electronicky things while his wife (wo)mans the store. We had stopped by several times to be told, "He'll be back at 7… at 8 … at 8:30 … you can catch him tomorrow." When we finally caught him and he heard how much we had pumped into that Internet device he almost hit the roof and told us NOT to put any more money into it. He took it and said he would find out what was wrong. He never did and that was the end of the Internet that summer. On a side note, our friends Steve and Tom have the same device and swear by it, yet our other friend Diane had exactly the same issue we did. Go figure.

    Needless to say, the following year I told Nick in no

uncertain terms that we HAD to get WIRED IN Internet, which meant going with Telecom Italia. Telecom Italia has an infamous reputation amongst the foreign community, so, thinking that all we had to do was get ahead of the game, we emailed MyHouse and asked them to arrange for Telecom Italia to set up the Wi-Fi for us before we arrived. We landed in Cianciana on July 3rd. No Wi-Fi.

MyHouse informed us that Telecom would arrive on the 9th to set up the Wi-Fi. Not so bad – less than a week. The 9th came and went – no Telecom. We called MyHouse who called Telecom. Telecom asked if we had a phone line in our house previously. MyHouse said no and Telecom said that in that case, they needed to send out two technicians and then they assured us that we would see them on Monday, Tuesday or Wednesday. I said to Nick, "You know this means we will see them on Thursday, right?" only half joking. No sign of them Monday or Tuesday so I called MyHouse to confirm that they would arrive on Wednesday. Oh no. They couldn't come on Wednesday. Instead they would arrive on Monday the 20th between 9:30 and 10:30. On Thursday I said to Nick, "We've been hanging around the house waiting for Telecom too long. Let's go to the market in Ribera." And off we went to Ribera. We were happily wandering up and down the stalls in the market when my cell phone rang. "Hello?" I said, not yet being quite onto this '*Pronto*' thing. "Hello, Diane? This is Joe at MyHouse. Telecom is at your house. Can you let them in?" "I would but we're in Ribera." "Oh, okay, we will let them in for you." Joe very kindly said. Then he said, "Oh wait. Now they are saying that your balcony is too high and they need two technicians." Wait, didn't they say that already and still they sent out one guy? Hmmmm. They promised to return the next morning (Friday). Of course they didn't show. At this point we started researching and phoning other companies. We decided to wait until Monday to see if they would show up between 9:30 and 10:30 as they had promised at one point. Guess what... Yup, no show. We called MyHouse to say that we were done with Telecom and were going to go with another company. Joe informed us that the technicians who installed for Telecom also installed for all the communications companies and to go with another company would mean getting bumped to the end of the line again. AARRGHHHH!!! So, once again, MyHouse called Telecom Italia and this time told them that we were ~~PISSED~~ slightly irate. "Okay," they said. "We will arrive on Tuesday. *Cento percento* (100%)".

Tuesday morning arrived and – miracle of freaking miracles – there they were! Two guys with a ladder! One of them came in and said something to Nick faster than I could follow but I could read the expression on Nick's face. "What is it?" I said with apprehension. "They can install the phone today but not the Internet." I could feel myself beginning to turn red. "*Quando?*" I asked the technician. "When?" He shrugged. "*Non lo so. Forse due settimane.*" Two weeks? Two weeks! I suddenly became like every Looney Tunes character that ever exploded on screen all rolled into one. "*Due settimane? Noi aspettiamo per OTTO GIORNI PER VOI!!! OTTO GIORNI!!!*" (We waiting for 8 days for you! 8 days!). "*NO DUE SETTIMANE. DOMANI!!!*" (No two weeks! Tomorrow!) "*No signora, non posso. Forse due settimane.*" (No ma'am, it's not possible. Maybe two weeks." "*NO!!! DOMANI!!!*" "*Non posso.*" "*NO NON POSSO! DOMANI DOMANI DOMANI!!!*" This was followed by a string of quite rude expletives in English from me that translate quite well into most languages. At this point Mr. Technician dialed his cell and, half suspecting that he was calling the *carabinieri* (Italian police) to cart off this crazy foreign lady, I thought 'Hmph, two can play at that game.' I got my phone and I started to dial...who could I dial? MyHouse! I got Joe, long suffering and patient Joe, who agreed to talk to Mr. Technician. I thrust my phone in the technician's face. He talked to Joe who came back on the line and told me that Mr. Technician had called his head office and the Wi-Fi would now be connected today. Wow. It is amazing how things that are not possible suddenly become possible in the face of a raging, crazed menopausal foreign woman.

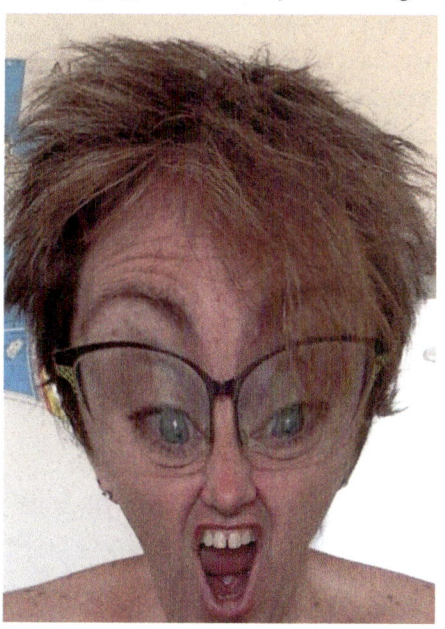

Now, I had heard all kinds of stories from different foreigners about Telecom including one couple in Cianciana

who had moved and were told that their phone and Wi-Fi could not be connected because their house did not exist. Didn't matter that the house was 100+ years old, as far as Telecom was concerned, their house did not exist. So, I started to do a little Internet research and in the space of less than 1 minute came up with dozens of stories of frustration over Telecom Italia, all of which made our experience look like a walk in an Italian park.
Deirdrè Straughan in her blog "Countries Beginning with I" said the following:

"...getting a phone line installed required a recommendation and a bottle of whiskey. The recommendation would ideally be from someone with contacts inside Telecom Italia, to ask the folks there to be nice to you. The bottle of whiskey would be a "gift" to encourage the technicians to get their job done, but you might need another bottle to tide you through the months-long, completely unnecessary wait!"

and...

"No one deals with Telecom Italia any more than they have to, because the service is so horrifically incompetent as to leave strong men weeping in frustration."

Rebecca Winke in her blog "Slow Travel Stories" said the following about getting her phone service back after a month with no phone, fax or Wi-Fi:

"...all of the sudden I am feeling all warm and fuzzy towards Telecom and beginning to understand that whole psychology behind why hostage victims begin to empathize

with their captors."

And finally, I can't even begin to quote from Pecora Nera's blog, "An Englishman in Italy". His story is so long, involved and funny that you just have to read it for yourself. Go to englishmaninitaly.org and search Telecom Italia. Trust me, it is well worth the read.

So, where does Amazon fit in to all this? While I was writing the original blog post describing our adventures with Telecom Italia, the doorbell rang. I hung over the rail of our 3rd floor terrazza to see the Amazon.it delivery guy standing at our door with a parcel for me. I had ordered the book less than a week before. Amazon emailed me and said it would arrive on July 27th. What day was it then? Miraculously, it was July 22nd. In my humble opinion, Telecom Italia should just be handed over to Amazon.it. Maybe everyone would actually get the service wanted, requested and required when they say they will deliver it or even before! I may just start a Facebook / Twitter campaign...

#switchTelecom4Amazon!

What book was I waiting for? One of my Sicily blogger colleagues, Veronica di Grigoli, and the person who very kindly wrote the introduction to this book, had published a new book: *The Dangerously Truthful Diary of a Sicilian Housewife.* As an expat married to a real born-and-raised-in-Sicily Sicilian, her perspective is a little different than mine and her book, very funny, is also well worth the read.

"Who has a priest at home, has plenty of food."
Sicilian Proverb

Spaghetti with Garlic Sauce

Ingredients:

about 1 pound of spaghetti
1/2 cup of olive oil
2 tbsp. of butter
4 heaping tbsp. of minced garlic (add more or less according to your taste)
1/4 cup finely chopped parsley
1 tsp. of dried basil and same again of dried oregano
Salt and pepper
grated parmesan

Directions:

Put spaghetti into a large pot of boiling salted water and cook until *al dente* (a little firm).
While the spaghetti is cooking, heat oil on medium heat in a frying pan.
Add garlic and parsley and keep stirring while it cooks to avoid burning.
As soon as the garlic and parsley are cooked, add the basil and oregano, continuing to stir.
Add butter and stir just long enough for the butter to melt then remove pan from heat.
Drain pasta and replace into the pot. Pour the oil/garlic/herb mixture over the pasta.

Add salt and pepper and parmesan to taste and then stir together until the parmesan is completely mixed in.
Serve right away while it is still hot. Place the parmesan on the table so each guest can add more if they wish.

Serves 4.

Chapter Sixteen
Crazy Mice Salad

As I have mentioned, my husband, and love of my life, is Sicilian. Or to be more accurate, he is Sicilian-Canadian, but as he is only one generation away from the old country, he feels the pull of the ancients perhaps more strongly than those of us whose families have been in Canada for multiple generations. As Nick and I are now creeping closer and closer to being ancients ourselves, we try to spend more and more time in the land of his ancestors. Every summer, we pack up our lives and climb on Air Canada, Lufthansa, British Airways or whichever carrier is the cheapest and fly our way, eventually, to Palermo's Punta Raisa Airport.

There is no feeling quite like that of circling Punta Raisa. On one side are the sparkling diamonds that float on the surface of the brilliantly azure Mediterranean, reflecting back the golden sun that sits proudly on his throne in the equally brilliant Sicilian sky. Nearby stands Mount Pellegrino glowing her warm terracotta colours and waiting for us to touch down. Every summer, Nick and I wriggle impatiently like roly-poly puppies, unable to contain our excitement at being back again on this island that captures our hearts over and over again.

Whenever we return to our village, Cianciana, we feel in many ways, as if we had never left. The house is usually in tip-top shape, mainly thanks to our good friend Franca who gives the house a thorough once over before we arrive. Somehow, the windows and doors manage to keep out the dust and sand that blows across the sea from the Sahara, although the pigeons invariably leave their mark on both *terrazze*.

Part of the charm of coming back to a small, friendly town like Cianciana is that everyone remembers you. People that we had interacted with in our first Sicilian summer, people I never expected to remember us, come up and said hello and welcome back and how long are you here for... It is a very warm feeling to know that we have made our own small mark in this town. One particular year, when we got off the bus from Palermo, the first person we saw was Angelo, from the Bar San Antonio. He smiled, waved and welcomed us back to Cianciana. We sat down and ordered two *arancini.* As we sat on the street, bags tucked beside our table, Franca and Pat came down the road and met us, proclaiming that now we had arrived, summer had officially started. We are grateful to be part of a community of Sicilians and Italians, Canadians, Brits, Poles and Americans, people from Belgium, France, Ireland, Denmark and oh so many other places. It is one of the gifts of such a place that we are welcomed into the global community.

The first week is always about getting caught up with friends and finding out how everyone has spent the past few months. Who got married, had a baby, died, moved? Who is on the outs with whom and who has taken over the family business? Who are the new foreigners in town? Which houses have sold? Which businesses have moved premises? And, most importantly, how are all our friends faring. On the first Sunday that year, Nick and I bumped our car down Doug's driveway. Doug is an expat from Vancouver – another Canadian in Cianciana. He and his brother bought seven acres of trees – olives, lemons, oranges, pomegranates – and a dilapidated little house. Well, the house is no longer dilapidated, the driveway that was once almost impassable is now partially paved and they have even built a small swimming pool. We made our trek to his house to invite him to join us on a drive to Sciacca.

Sciacca is a port city – the largest city in the region of Agrigento – with a marina filled with fishing boats. It is famous for two things really – ceramics and incredibly fresh fish. And Jon Bon Jovi's dad. He was born and raised in

Sciacca. Not really a huge tourist draw, I'm thinking. What took us to Sciacca on that Sunday, however, was the fish. A fresh fish dinner in Sciacca had been on my 'to do' list ever since our first visit, years before, and on that particular day, we decided to make it happen. We followed the road down to the dock. Restaurants abound everywhere in Sicily and Sciacca is no different. In the block from where we parked our battered little car to the fishing boats, we passed three restaurants ranging from a little *mamma e papá* place to what was obviously a high end and quite expensive establishment complete with waiters in white shirts, black vests and bow ties serving wine on the *terrazza* to Armani suited patrons. Not exactly our style. The best way to find a good restaurant, of course, is to ask someone local, and the best way to find a good fish restaurant is to ask a local fisherman.

Two fishermen tossing huge bags of ice from a truck up onto the deck of their fishing vessel pointed us to Ristorante Porto San Paolo. Our gaze followed theirs up to a restaurant at the top of a rock immediately beside us. As I said, who better to trust about a fish restaurant than a fisherman?

It was everything I hoped for. The view was stunning, the fish was very good and the company was pleasant. Our waiter even spoke English, of a sort. And the English menu was filled with various odd translations of either the names or descriptions of Sicilian fish dishes. For the most part, we were able to figure out what each one meant until we got to Crazy Salad. That was it. No other description, just Crazy Salad. Nick called the waiter over and asked in Sicilian what is Crazy Salad? The waiter responded in something close to English: *Radicchio*, tomatoes, mushrooms, *mozzarella*, *pecorino*, and… mice. Mice? Surely he didn't mean… mice? I asked the waiter, Mice??? *Certo*? *Sí, sí*. Mice, mice. Okay. I'm up for a challenge. *Un* Crazy Salad *per favore*.

Now, you have to understand, I am fine with spiders. Snakes don't bother me at all. Lizards running up and down the wall, I find rather cute. But rodents? No, I am not fond of mice, rats or anything of that ilk. I'm the 'jump on the table screaming' type when it comes to mice. So why did I order the Crazy Salad with Mice? Only the ancient Sicilian gods know. Perhaps I like to live on the edge. No, that's definitely not it. Momentary fit of madness? More likely. As I sat and watched Nick and Doug sip their wine and talk about house renos and Sicilian bureaucracy, I fixated on my Mice Salad. Would the mice come laid out across the top of the *radicchio*? Would there be little morsels hidden within the salad? Would there be little deep fried mice drumsticks? My anxiety level was growing. What if I couldn't face it? Could I pick through the salad and just leave the mouse McNuggets on the side? Would that be rude? What is the etiquette for a mouse salad? Nick, knowing my aversion to rodents, had simply raised his eyebrows at me when I'd ordered but wisely said nothing when I defiantly met his gaze. However, he knew me well enough to know what I was thinking. When the waiter came out of the kitchen carrying our plates of food, Nick quietly began singing the Jaws theme song… dum dum…dum dum…dum dum… and then just before the waiter arrived a quick crescendo of dum dum daaaaa! The waiter placed our fish dishes on the table and my salad in front of me. I smiled wanly at him, picked up my fork and started fishing through the salad for bits of rodent. Well, there was definitely *radicchio*. Mushrooms. *Mozzarella*. Corn. Wait. Corn? The waiter hadn't said corn. And what is corn in Sicilian? *Mais*. OMG. The ball dropped. It wasn't MICE that the waiter had said but *MAIS*. I had been having a panic attack over a CORN salad. Nick sat smirking beside me. He knew exactly what the salad was and exactly what I had been thinking. "Don't…say…a word." I muttered to him under my breath and took a mouthful of what was a very uneventful CORN salad.

"The oranges of the island are like blazing fire among emerald boughs."
Abd ar-Rahman of Trapani, Sicilian-Arab poet, Court of Roger II

Sicilian Orange Salad

Ingredients:

4 large oranges (I use 4 large navel oranges but you can use any kind of orange. I think a mixture of blood oranges

with navel oranges would be nice.)

½ lemon

¼ red onion

sea salt

sicilian olives, pitted

olive oil

Directions:

Peel the oranges and 1/2 lemon and cut them into large chunks and placed them in a bowl.
Dice the onion and olives and add to the bowl.
Pour olive oil to taste over the ingredients – at least 3-4 tablespoons.
Let sit at room temperature for 15-30 minutes to allow the orange juice and oil to mix.
Add salt to taste.

Serves 4.

Chapter Seventeen
Medieval Monkey Business

One day I was out walking with my husband. We had one of those glorious winter days that we are sometimes gifted with on Vancouver Island. The sky was pale blue with little white clouds floating stationary above us. Walking down the street, I had to squint against the bright sun reflecting off the frosty lawns. The air was cold but so clean that when I filled my lungs I could almost feel the oxygen flushing toxins out of my cells.

We walked along our quiet road on that Sunday in our little Island hamlet looking at all the Christmas decorations already up and it brought me back to a moment last summer in another little island hamlet.

Last summer, I got a Facebook message from my friend, Linda:

Hey, what are you doing on Aug 16th?

Recovering from Ferragosto. Why?

You HAVE to come and stay with us in Buccheri.

Sure. Why?

They are throwing Medfest.

Medfest? What's that?

Crazy medieval festival – jugglers, costumes, lots of drinking, lots of food and men – straight men – in tights throwing flags.

Men in tights? I'm in!!!!!

So, on the morning of August 16th we found ourselves packed into our little smartcar and on the road to the other side of Sicily and Buccheri, a little mountain town in Siracusa.

After a couple of side trips and a parking lot of a traffic jam on the way into Catania, we found ourselves pulling in to Buccheri after dark. Bruno, Linda's husband, met us and drove our little car with Nick to find a place to park while I walked down the hill to meet Linda in the piazza.
The piazza was chock full of people – locals, tourists, people in costumes, people laughing, singing, dancing and – above all – eating. Every inch of street side was filled with stalls and kiosks selling all kinds of medieval food – mostly meat. Roasted horsemeat, wild boar, sausages, and other meats that I couldn't identify. And wine. Wine everywhere. It was a raucous, crazy, block party à la Giovanni Boccaccio's Decameron or Chaucer's Canterbury Tales.

After stuffing ourselves with horsemeat and sausages, we wandered through the crowds, stopping to see the churches that were decked out in all kinds of medieval displays.

We spent the night in Linda and Bruno's Airbnb, a gorgeous apartment high on the edge of the town looking out over the whole of Buccheri. We got up in the morning and wandered from one side of the town to the other, stopping at the *piazza* for breakfast (*gelato* in a brioche and a *cappuccino*) and eventually stumbling across the best restaurant in town where we dined on roasted wild boar and snails big enough to fill a soup spoon.

On a side note, as we wandered, we kept bumping into the same group of 4 Italian tourists. At one point, one of the men approached us and asked Nick if he were an actor. Nick shook his head and the man told us that his group was sure he was a famous English movie star! They couldn't remember the name of the star but I'm thinking it must have been Gary Oldman as Sirius Black.

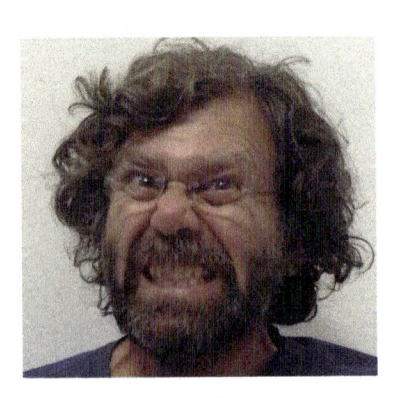

A nap in the afternoon and we were ready to go again. Linda, Bruno, Nick and I made our way through the rapidly growing crowds to see the displays of acrobats, fire dancers and (of all things) Irish folk bands. Stalls of goods for sale from traditional handicrafts to kitschy junk from China and Taiwan spread up and down streets all over the town. At three in the morning we stopped at a food stall just around the corner from the apartment and sat on some stairs eating *cannoli* filled with warm, sweet *ricotta* and sharing stories with Linda and Bruno.

We said goodnight to our hosts, and just before we opened the door to the apartment, Linda reminded us to leave on the outside lights to keep away any drunken revelers from treating their doorstep as a convenient urinal (apparently a common occurrence during Medfest).

Medfest was an exciting, exuberant bacchanalian party. This is not normally our kind of celebration, but there was something so joyously adolescent about this unruly and boisterous festival that we vowed we would come back again next year. And we suggest that you do too.

"When you see a sheep's wool sky you know, if it doesn't rain today, it will rain in the morning."
Sicilian Proverb

Ragusa Lamb Pie

Ingredients:

1 package pre-made bread dough
2 pounds of boneless lamb
3 onions

1 tbsp. of tomato paste
½ cup red wine
1 egg
olive oil

Directions:

Defrost the bread dough in a plastic bag in the microwave for about 5 minutes.
Preheat the oven to 170F.
Place the dough on a plate in the oven, turn off the heat and leave for 60-90 minutes.
Chop onions into small pieces then brown in oil in the fry pan.
Add the pieces of lamb to the pan then pour in the red wine and cook until it evaporates.
Mix 1 tbsp. of tomato paste into a cup of hot water and add to the pan.
Season with sea salt and pepper.
Cover and cook for 10 minutes then remove the lid and continue to cook for 10 minutes, reducing the liquid by ½ – ¾.
Oil the baking dish and then spread half the dough on the bottom.
Pour the stew onto the dough in the baking dish and cover with the other half of the dough, pinching the edges together.
Poke holes in the top with a fork and then brush with one beaten egg yoke.
Bake in a hot oven (425F – 450F) for 20-30 minutes.

Serves 4 - 6.

Chapter Eighteen
Ferragosto

One of the best things for me about having a house in another part of the world is the fast and very tight friendships you make. Of those friendships, one of the best we have made as a couple is with Linda and Bruno. I met Linda online in one of the myriad of expat forums. I liked her straightforward and down-to-earth personality immediately. And it doesn't hurt that she can be uproariously funny. She is married to Bruno, a Sicilian from the very trendy island of Ortigia, just off Syracuse. I've seen pictures of Bruno as a young man, and he looked like a young Marlon Brando although Linda swears he looked more like a young Elvis.

Linda and Bruno live in the hills on the east side of Sicily and have very kindly put us up whenever we make our way out to that side of the island. One summer we slept on a pullout bed on their covered *terrazza*. In the middle of the night there was a thunder and lightening storm and the rain came pelting down, the way it does in Sicily - no half measures on our island. It was amazing. We had the experience of being out in the middle of a wild thunder and lightning storm without being caught in the downpour. As we lay snuggled up in our bed we watched the skylight up and shivered as the thunder crashed overhead. Eventually the storm passed and we went back to sleep, but when I woke up early in the morning, I was met with spectacular skies and cactus drenched with rain. It felt like a gift from the storm gods.

That day was Ferragosto, one of the most important holidays in Italy. It celebrates the ascension of Mary into heaven and most towns have a procession in which they carry a statue of Mary around the town. We had been in the crowds in Cianciana following the procession of Mary but that year we did something new. We climbed into Linda and Bruno's van and drove up to Palazzolo Acreide, a lovely little town in the lavish baroque style of the Spanish invaders and had lunch sitting on the balcony of the restaurant and watching the few people out on the street in the midday sun dart back and forth, trying to maximize the shade. Later, we drove farther into the hills and stopped once again in Buccheri, the small town we had visited for Medfest built in the depression of a long dead volcano and well renown for the excellence of their olive oil. We sat in the *piazza*, sipping on cold drinks and fighting the heat with the sweet and ubiquitous *gelato*. Finally, we drove down to the beach in Avola. Linda and I stripped down to our swimsuits while Nick and Bruno went off in search of swordfish pizza. Linda and I swam in the dark, floating and looking up at the millions of stars as they danced across the sky above us, and listening to plop plop of fish jumping up from the sea around us. When Nick and Bruno returned with the pizza, we sat on the beach eating our dinner and listening to the people down the beach singing; from modern tunes to Italian folk music and all in a similarly tone deaf manner. And yet it didn't matter. It was all wonderful.

After we said goodbye to Linda and Bruno, we moved on to a cabin that we had rented for when Nick's sister and brother-in-law visited us from Canada. The cabin was in Acireale, a small city on the north side of Catania. When we arrived at the cabin we were delighted to discover that it was on the edge of a plant nursery filled with palm trees and cacti. On the other side, the cabin sat on the edge of a cliff face and next to it was a large well with a spiral staircase that took you deep into the heart of the cliff. At the bottom was a tunnel with a large metal door at the end. When the door was opened, you stepped out onto a platform just above where the cliff face met the sea. Stairs took you down to the black volcanic rock and the sea so warm that you barely felt the water as you stepped in. As we looked out, we could see fishermen in their small boats fishing in the same ancient ways that their ancestors had fished as well as wealthy families holidaying in their flashy powerboats and yachts. Nick and I floated out from the shoreline and peered up at the top of the cliff and wondered at the resiliency of the cacti that seemed to be able to grow out of the most inhospitable locations. So far below the cabins and the workers in the nursery, all we could hear was the water lapping against the rocks. It was utter peace, floating in the soft, salty warm bath that is the Ionian Sea.

On our way back to Cianciana we stopped in Caltagirone, a town famous for ceramics. We poked through the shops and I picked up a couple of little pieces for our kitchen. I like going into the various ceramics towns because, although they all have similarly styled items, each town has its own unique offerings. One thing that makes Caltagirone famous is the tiled staircase. It goes waaaaaaaay up and every step face is tiled with a differently decorated tile. Nick and I spent our afternoon poking through the little ceramics shops that line the *piazza* on either side of the staircase. In the back of one of the shops I found a little blue, green and yellow cat that reminded me of my friend Pat's little kitten, Zoe. After paying, I tucked my find carefully into my purse to bring home as a little surprise for Pat. We finished our afternoon sitting in the shade of a street-side cafè sharing a *gelato* and sipping on lemonade. It was perfect way to watch the afternoon wane, observing the relaxed smile on Nick's face and appreciating the gifts that this generous island had given us.

"Better to be born a limpet in the sea, than a load bearing donkey."
Sicilian proverb

Sicilian Octopus Salad

Ingredients:

3 cups of cooked octopus cut up, approximately 1" cubes (body) or 2" lengths (legs)
5 tsp. minced garlic
1-½ cups finely chopped red onion

2 tbsp. chopped basil
1 tbsp. chopped parsley
½ tsp. sea salt
1 tsp. ground garlic pepper
¼ - ½ tsp. of red pepper seeds (optional)
1 bay leaf
½ cup olive oil
3 tbsp. fresh lemon juice

Directions:

Mix octopus, garlic, red onion, basil, parsley, red pepper seeds and bay leaf in a mixing bowl.
Put the olive oil, lemon juice and ¼ tsp. sea salt in a jar with a tight lid and shake vigorously.
Pour over octopus and onion mixture.
Place in refrigerator and marinate for at least 4 hours.
Just before serving, remove the bay leaf and shake the remaining sea salt and pepper over the salad.

Serves 5.

Chapter Nineteen
Driving Life's Back Roads

Back in 1974, the Americans had just exited Vietnam, the era of free love was ending, disco was on the horizon, and I was visiting Sicily for the first time. It was also the year that Robert Pirsig published *Zen and the Art of Motorcycle Maintenance* and turned the razor's edge of Phaedrus' intellect into a prodigious instrument measuring the metaphysics of quality.The metaphor of the motorcycle road trip was a perfect vehicle to talk about living a life defined by experiences instead of a life defined by acquisitions – quality of time versus quantity of stuff. Pirsig wrote about the superiority of 'twisty hilly roads' empty of traffic, lined with meadows and orchards. Hmmm. Sounds like Sicily.

Zoom forward to 1981 when I first read *Zen and the Art of Motorcycle Maintenance* for a creative writing class at UBC. The University of British Columbia is in Vancouver, Canada's third largest city and the place where I grew up. I didn't really 'get' the whole *Zen* thing. And *Motorcycle Maintenance* was far beyond my ken. I was commuting to and from school and work 2 hours every day, and working 7 days a week to pay for my tuition and books and car which meant driving through some of the worst traffic in Canada. I had lived in the rush and bustle my whole life. The heady days of the 60's and early 70s were gone and the Yuppies were claiming their thrones. My professor was a leftover hippie – and I mean this now in the very best possible way. He was trying to make us think, to evaluate, to see that life was much more than what was on the surface. I was too busy for that. Ironically, I wanted a creative writing professor to give me the 'rules' and I would follow those rules and thus become a good, if not great, writer. Eventually I dropped his class and waited another semester to join another creative writing class with a professor who was more conventional and didn't push me to think as much. At the time I thought he was much better. Now I realize what a gift the first professor was, I just wasn't ready for the kind of introspection that he was trying to engender in his students. It would be easy to fall into regrets over this loss of opportunity however, as my very dear friend Neil frequently says: "Everything is exactly as it's meant to be."

At the time, my goal was to graduate as quickly as I could manage, get a teaching job, bump up the ladder and retire as the principal of some large Vancouver high school with loads of money and a nice house near Spanish Banks (a long sandy beach with gorgeous views of the mountains) alongside my equally successful doctor husband and two beautiful children who were finishing their degrees at my alma mater – one in something artistic like sculpture or creative writing, and the other in some brainiac major like neuro-psycho-environmental-chemo-biophysics. They would become world famous in their fields and would eventually bring their equally beautiful and brilliant children to visit Grandmama and Grandpapa.

Well, as anyone over the age of 35 knows, these dreams of our youth – especially the highly specific ones like mine – rarely turn out the way we expect. I graduated in 1983 when the newly elected government of British Columbia decimated education. In my cohort of 60 students graduating with a B.Ed. in English Education, I believe only three of us actually made it into the classroom with one other returning to teaching 20 years later for a brief stint.

Four out of sixty. I applied to jobs everywhere. I sent out over 150 resumes and had three interviews. I even applied to a job 250 miles north of Edmonton and didn't even get a response. Finally, out of desperation, I applied to a teaching job in Japan and got hired.

The 1980s was the time to be in the land of the rising sun. The sun kept on rising and rising and business got better and better and the money just flowed. The funny thing was, once I got there, the race for the dollar – or the yen in that case – ceased to be the important thing. I was part of a subculture of foreign English teachers. There was no race for the top because, as foreign teachers we were, for the most part, as high as we could go in our language schools, high schools or junior colleges. There was no more pressure to succeed – we were there. We started looking for other things to fill our time – and we had lots of spare time. We lived in little apartments with *tatami* mats made of rice straw on the floor. We took our shoes off without fail when we entered our houses. We visited temples and shrines and prayed to whatever gods happened to be there even though few of us were Buddhist and none of us were Shinto. We drank and partied. We went to outdoor hot springs and sat naked under the stars in the steaming water sipping hot sake or cold beer. Some of us climbed Mt Fuji, others surfed the waves in Chiba, others studiously memorized the crazy symbols known as *kanji* or learned tea ceremony, and still others sat under cherry trees out in full blossom and wrote mostly bad haiku. Without thinking about it, we were learning to embrace the idea of good time to which Pirsig referred.

So, at this point you are probably thinking, what the hell

does all of this have to do with Sicily? Everything. At least, everything for me. In early 2015, I decided that it was almost time to pack in my career (by the way, I never became principal, worked in Vancouver or married a doctor and my daughter and husband are far superior to any imaginings that came out of my overactive twenty-something brain). No more commuting, after-school staff meetings or parent-teacher interviews for me. When I hit 55 I retired within days. I turned in my notice, told my principal and all my colleagues – there was no turning back, even if I wanted to. This meant that I could spend more time in our beloved Cianciana.

This is the place that Pirsig was talking about, even if he had never heard anything about Sicilian village life. The back roads of Sicily are winding, making their way around mountains and hills, bays and coves. On the road from Cianciana to Ribera, olive trees, orange trees, figs, pears, plums and grapevines reach out as if to say "Pick me, pick me!" and we almost could by simply reaching our hands out of the passenger windows. The mountains roll down to the edge of the road, coming to a halt to let drivers pass by, and cliffs drop precariously on the other side. Nick and I drive these roads with joy. And if by chance we get lost, the easiest thing in the world is to stop in a little village – we know we will find one if we drive long enough – go into the bar in the heart of the town, order *il caffè* and ask for directions. They will give us directions to somewhere. It might be the place we are looking for or it could be somewhere else entirely. Actually it will most likely be somewhere else entirely, but wherever it is, it will be interesting.

Occasionally it is frustrating but even then it makes good fodder for stories later on. Sicily is made up of good time if you let it happen. The mechanic that promised our car back this morning? Well, now he is saying tomorrow afternoon. This is a chance to sit and sip coffee with our new friend from California or to practice my Italian with our neighbour Antonio or to catch up on all the village gossip with my other Ciancianesi friends. Telecom didn't show to hook up our Internet on the day they promised? Well, we spent the day reading or writing or learning new Italian words from the language books we brought so that we can use the new words later on in the *piazza*. In many ways, it seems that the ancient gods and the politicians of Sicily conspire to slow everyone down, whether they like it or not. Roads are dotted with "Caution! 20 km/hr!" signs that are placed before tiny bumps in the road and enormous suspension breaking, car swallowing potholes. Your choice is to fly over them all at break neck speed and hope that they are all little bumps or to relax and assume they will all be the giant potholes. Again, the **good** time versus the good **time**. In April 2015, a bridge on the Palermo-Catania autostrada – the main highway that passes through the heart of Sicily – collapsed. The newspapers screamed that the politicians are not keeping up the roadways. They are corrupt! What are they doing! All these things are likely true and now we have a major autostrada that is closed for months or, more likely, years. *Deus ex machina* in the form of politicians. So, for the foreseeable future, Sicilians will be forced to take the slower, windier routes. As frustrating as this may be, it isn't necessarily a bad thing. In the very best aspects of Sicily, the pace is slower. I tell my friend from California I will be at her house in 20 minutes so we can go shopping together but the heat is oppressive and it takes me 40. I joke with her that it was a Sicilian 20 minutes and we both laugh, not at anyone in particular but in appreciation of how different our lives are here than when we are back in North America. The best of living in Sicily is truly driving life's back roads.

"To have seen Italy without having seen Sicily is not to have seen Italy at all, for Sicily is the clue to everything."
Goethe

Spaghetti with Fried Zucchini

Ingredients:

Enough spaghetti for 2 people
2 smallish zucchini
2 tsp. minced garlic or to taste
grated parmesan to taste

sea salt to taste
fresh ground pepper to taste
olive oil
capers to taste (optional)

Directions:

Slice zucchini thinly.
Heat the olive oil in a pan and stir in minced garlic.
Add zucchini, pinch of salt and capers if desired and fry.
Remove from the heat when the zucchini has a nice toasty colour.
Boil spaghetti *al dente* while zucchini are frying and arrange in the serving bowl.
Pour zucchini with garlic oil over the pasta, and toss.
Add pepper and grated parmesan.

Serves 2.

Chapter Twenty
Gifts from *La Cucina*

In June of 2016, I decided that it was time I actually tried to fill some of the holes in my lacklustre Italian so I registered with Scuola Virgilio, packed my bags and boarded a flight to Trapani. After hours in the air, I found myself situated in a lovely apartment that is owned by the very intelligent and beautiful Annalisa and very quick and witty Tommaso. They were patient with my slow and sometimes unintelligable Italian and my struggles to understand but we did manage to have some very interesting conversations while Tommaso cooked.

Annalisa is an Italian history teacher and Tommaso is an actor. I assumed he was a struggling actor as almost all the actors I know are exactly that. He told me that he mainly acted in films. Nick and I try to watch Italian and Sicilian films whenever we can so I asked him which ones he had been part of. To my astonishment, he told me he had been in *Baarìa, Il Dolce e L'Amaro, I Cento Passi,* all films that I had seen. Not only that, he was in the supporting role in *Lo Scambio,* the opening film to the 33rd Torino International Film Festival. These are all big name, well-reviewed and well-respected films. I was suitably impressed. It didn't take long, however, for me to realize how down-to-earth both Tommaso and Annalisa truly are.

During my time in Trapani I realized that if I were to omit a chapter on the dishes that Sicilians have created for themselves at home I would be truly amiss. I began to ask people I met, 'what do you cook at home?' Some simply laughed me off. Some would tell me what they made but not how they made it. But some, well some told me amazing, wonderful things that they cook for themselves regularly: amazing fish dishes, dishes with pistachio and cream, rice with smoked fish, and light fresh vegetable dishes.

One afternoon, I wandered into a little shop, *Sicilia Bedda*. *Bedda* means beautiful in Sicilian and beautiful it was. They had such a selection of typical Sicilian and *trapanese* foods that my mouth watered just walking in. I started up a conversation with a friendly sales clerk who introduced herself to me as Maristella. It was the perfect name for a lovely young woman from a city surrounded by the Mediterranean. You see, Maristella means 'Star of the Sea'. She pointed out the different kinds of sea salt, pestos and a wonderful thing that was like Nutella but made with pistachios! It was ridiculously delicious. I waved vaguely in the direction of all of the varieties of pistachio and asked her what she would do with them. I could see the wheels turning as she considered which dish to share. This turned out to be a pasta dish that sounded (and later tasted) delicious.

> **"The mouse said to the nut; give me time and I shall reach you."**
> **Sicilian Proverb**

Tommaso Caporrimo's Fresh Zucchini

Ingredients

2 small and tender zucchini
lemon juice
6 or 7 very thinly sliced lemon slices
olive oil
freshly ground pepper

Directions

Using either a sharp vegetable peeler or a spiralizer, slice the 2 zucchini as close to paper thin as possible.
Put the zucchini and the lemon slices in a plastic container with a sealing lid.
Add equal parts of lemon juice and olive oil, just enough to coat the zucchini.
Seal the cover and shake then let sit for 20-30 minutes.
Plate the zucchini and then sprinkle with sea salt and pepper to taste.

Serves 4

Maristella Mazzara's Pistachio Pasta

Ingredients

farfalle (bowtie) pasta - enough for 4 people
5 - 6 pieces of bacon
3/4 cup of pistachio pesto
1/4 cup of *panna di cucina* or (if outside Italy) unsweetened whipping cream
2 tbsp. small pieces of pistachio
salt and pepper

Directions

Boil farfalle according to the instructions.
Cook bacon until crispy and then crumble.

Mix pesto, bacon and panna together and then mix into the pasta.
Sprinkle with small pieces of pistachio.
Season with salt and pepper to taste.

Serves 4.

Chapter Twenty-five
The Original Multicultural Society

The sun brightened what was an unseasonably warm October 15th. My hand was still swollen from the yellowjacket sting that had demonstrated, two days before, the unfortunate fact that I have an anaphylactic allergy to the little bastards. I winced as I unthinkingly slammed the car door with that hand. My right hand. Of course. I shrugged my purse higher onto my shoulder and ambled over to the coffee shop door. This was, what, the 15th? 16th? 20th? blind date since I started Internet dating. I wasn't particularly hopeful but neither was I discouraged. It would be whatever it would be and at the very least I would have a latte out of it. I started to reach for the door, stopped myself and switched to my left hand. As I did, I turned slightly to the right and glanced through the plate glass window. I stopped. He had lovely brown curly hair. He had kind grey eyes. He had a shy, hopeful look. 'Gawd I hope that's him.' I thought to myself.

Well, you may have guessed – this was my first glimpse

of Nick. We sat in the coffee shop and talked for two hours and it would have been longer had I not had a doctor's appointment to deal with my ridiculous stung hand. As we talked, he told me that he was from Ottawa, he worked as an educational assistant, and that he was not just Italian, but Sicilian.

Really? Nick did not look anything like my mental image of a Sicilian. What was my mental image? A young Al Pacino from The Godfather perhaps? Maybe Ray Liotta in Good Fellows? Certainly I expected black hair, dark eyes and olive skin. Nick had none of these things. He told me that the family joke was that he must have been fathered by the milkman because he was born almost platinum blonde. Two years later when I finally met Nick's family in Ottawa, his sister Tina, surprised me with her black hair and dark brown eyes. Both Nick's parents had black hair, dark eyes and olive skin and both his parents were tall; very atypical for Sicilians. Nick's Uncle Giacomo has Nick's colouring, yet is diminutive. In my crazy mixed up family, these kinds of traits are to be expected; yet Nick's entire family is not just Italian but Sicilian – how can this be? The truth of the matter is that any Sicilian you can think of has a lineage far more crazily mixed up than my own. The history of Sicily is fascinating – for any history nut, Sicily is like manna from heaven and to find out who are these people who call themselves Sicilians is a puzzle worthy of any true history buff.

Sicily is a bit of an enigma. Sicilians are Italian but are they really closer to mainland Italians than they are to North Africans? What about places like Piazza Armerina where the Sicilian spoken there is closer to French than Italian and the layout of the town would be familiar to anyone coming to visit from Normandy? Sicily may lay only three kilometres from the toe of the boot, but it is also a short 160 kilometres from North Africa. In some places Tunisia is farther north than Sicily. I wrote earlier in the chapter on salt, the strategic importance of Sicily. Because of this, Sicily has been invaded more times than anyone unfamiliar with her history can imagine.

The first Sicilians – the Indigenous people of the island – were the Sicanians. There is evidence of them going back in time as far as that of the First Peoples in North America. It was not long, however, before the Sicanians were sharing their home. Immigrants came to Sicily – some with a sword, some with an olive branch, but come they did. I am not an expert historian, only a history buff, but by my count there have been twenty invasions or migrations of various sorts to Sicily. Who were these invaders and migrants? They were (deep breath)...

Elymians...Sicels...Phoenicians...Greeks...Carthaginians...Romans...Vandals and Goths...Byzantines...Arabs...Normans...Swabians...Angevins...Aragonese...Albanians...Spanish...Jews...Germans...Allied Forces...Europeans from various member nations of the European Union...

But wait, you say. That is only nineteen! True. There is one more sweep of people into this mixed up history of invasion and migration and it is one that is ongoing still. It is of course, the desperate flood of refugees coming from Syria, other Middle Eastern countries and from all over Africa.

In modern times, Sicilians have been aware of the trafficking of North and Sub-Saharan Africans back and forth between the Sicilian island of Lampedusa and Libya since the year 2000. And, as always, nations play with the lives of those who live without privilege, power, and often hope.

Early in the 2000s, the Italian and Libyan governments made a secret deal in which Libya agreed to accept all African deportees from Italy, a secret deal that meant that by 2005 there was a mass repatriation across the Mediterranean. This return of unwanted immigrants to Libya helped build a lucrative illegal business – that of unscrupulous Libyan smugglers who took large sums of money to ferry desperate people in rickety boats back to the shores of Lampedusa. The numbers of refugees continued to grow until by 2009, the temporary refugee centre in Lampedusa was brimming with more than double the number of illegal migrants than it had originally been built to hold. The Arab Spring brought a whole new wave of migrants. By the end of August in 2011, over 48,000 refugees had arrived, mostly young men. Over the last five years, the waves of illegal immigrants into Sicily have been steadily increasing and making riskier and riskier crossings in the hopes of making a new life in Europe. Desperate refugees from Syria, Libya, Eritrea, Somalia, Pakistan and Palestine are fleeing to boats on the most dangerous migrant crossing in the world – over 1700 people perished in April 2015, the worst month overall in terms of loss of life.

To put the numbers in real perspective, over 11,000 migrants were rescued in the same time period meaning almost 13,000 people attempted to make the crossing from Libya to Sicily in that month that we know of.

So much about this saddens me. These people are so desperate to leave their homes – homes that they love; they will scrape together the equivalent of $1000 US each to climb aboard these unseaworthy vessels. And yet, the doors of so many European countries are slamming shut even though all evidence shows that refugees work harder and do better in the long term than many other immigrants.

Don't believe me on this last one? According to IIE (a field office of the US Committee for Refugees and Immigrants), "Strengthened by adversity, they make capable, resilient, and loyal employees." In Canada, the Victoria Immigrant and Refugee Centre Society says, "…the majority of these new arrivals bring positive working habits such as loyalty, hard working [sic], etc. to the new workplace…" Yet, in spite of all this, refugees struggle to find and keep work in their new countries.

On April 25, 2015, *The Economist* published an insightful article on the situation. The article calls for the European Union to change their policies on asylum (which have grown stricter since the publication of the article). That there is a lack of recognition to shelter these desperate refugees simply because they are people in dire straits underlines a breakdown of ethics within the EU. It points out that there are over one million migrants camped along the coast of north Africa and suggests that the best way to protect the lives of these refugees is to process them on the south shore of the Mediterranean before they climb into boats.

But to take this story from the global and focus again on the more personal perspective of Sicily, let me finish this chapter with one story. In Cianciana, if you walk down the hill from the old part of the town, and turn off onto Via Ugo Foscolo, you will pass the town cemetery. Walking through the gates and wandering up and down inside, you could be forgiven if you miss ten graves that are not marked with any Ciancianese family names. These graves contain the remains of ten of the migrants who perished in the tragedy of April 2015. These people had no family or friends in Cianciana. They had no ties at all but the good people of Cianciana could not see these poor refugees disposed of in an undignified way. They opened their hearts and made space for them in their little community, even if it was after death. I can't think of any story that would more thoroughly epitomize the kindnesses with which we have been gifted in our adopted Sicilian home.

**"Water does harm but wine makes you sing."
Sicilian Proverb**

Simplified Sicilian-style Couscous

Ingredients:

1 large onion
¼ cup of extra virgin olive oil
2 large cans diced tomatoes
1 large pinch of crushed red pepper flakes (or a little more if you desire)
1 tbsp. dried parsley
2 tbsp. minced garlic
2 tbsp. dried or minced basil
4 tbsp. of tomato paste
2 lbs. of halibut trimmings including bones
5 cups of cold water
Sea salt and ground pepper to taste
¼ tsp. turmeric
½ cup raisins
1 package couscous

Directions:

Put cold water into a large pot, followed by a little salt and the halibut. Other white fish could be used if halibut isn't available.
Slowly heat the water until it is simmering but do not let it get to a full, rolling boil.

Continue simmering until the flesh falls off the bone easily.

While the fish is simmering, heat the oil in a large sauté pan.

Add the onions and sauté until translucent, stirring continually.

Add the tomatoes and cook for 15 minutes more, stirring occasionally.

Season with salt, pepper and hot pepper flakes to taste.

Mix the parsley, basil, and minced garlic together.

Scoop the fish out of the broth with a slotted spoon.

Separate the fish from the bones and pull apart into small pieces.

Add the fish to the sauce.

Stir the tomato paste into the sauce.

Cover the pot and simmer on a very low heat for about 20 minutes.

Prepare the couscous according to package directions using the fish broth instead of water and adding turmeric and raisins.

Cover and remove pan from heat.

Let stand until grains are tender, about seven to ten minutes.

Uncover and stir the grains with fork.

Season with sea salt and ground pepper to taste.

Place the couscous on a large dish in a nicely formed mound.

Pour the sauce over half the couscous.

Put any leftover sauce in a gravy boat on the table.

Sprinkle with extra parsley if desired.

Serves 8.

Epilogue

"My house, my house! As small as you may be, to me you are a palace!"
Italian proverb

The sun goes down over Cianciana. Behind each of these doors, *Ciancianesi* families are sharing good Sicilian food and telling their stories of the day. Once dinner is done, as always, people meet in the *piazza* to do *passeggiata* together and to share a coffee or a glass of wine. Some conversation is jovial, some is in conspiratory whispers, some in loud disagreement. No matter what the emotion or conversation, both Sicilians and expats live here with passion for that is the lesson of this magical island. Sicily, for those of us that call Cianciana home; for those of us that call Sicily home, you will always be our palace.

Index

A
anchovies · 13
antipasto · 69
apples · 49
arancini · 34, 36, 76

B
beef · 41
bell peppers · 69
biscotti · 52
bread · 16, 51
bread dough · 112

C
caffè · 76, 81, 83, 122
caffè Americano · 77
caffè con panna · 77
caffè corretto · 77
caffè freddo · 77
caffè Hag · 77
caffè macchiato · 77
cannoli · 112
capers · 69
caponata · 69
cappuccino · 75, 77, 82, 110
cazzilli · 63-65
cheese, caciocavallo · 41, 64, 74
cheese, mozzarella · 36, 105-106
cheese, parmesan · 36, 64, 74, 124-125
cheese, pecorino · 41, 64,105
cheese, ricotta · 112
cheese, romano · 41
chicken · 41
chickpeas · 27, 91
chicory · 105, 106
cookies · 52
corn · 106-107
couscous · 136-137

E
eggplant · 69
eggs · 36, 56, 64
espresso · 75-79

F
fish · 104-106, 137
fritters · 27

G
garlic · 101, 117-118, 124, 137
gelato · 49, 76, 110, 116, 117
gluten · 86-90
granita · 78

H
ham · 36
horsemeat · 110

L
lamb · 41, 112
lemons · 13, 16, 32, 128
limoncello · 32

M

melons · 51
mint · 91
minni di virgini · 64

O

octopus · 117-118
olives · 13, 69, 122
oranges · 13, 107-108, 122

P

panelle · 27
pani ca' meusa · 39-40
pasta · 64, 129
peaches · 51
pesto · 36, 129
pine nuts · 69
pistachio · 129
pizza · 76, 85-86, 90, 116
pork · 16, 41
potatoes · 16, 64, 85

R

radicchio · 105, 106
rice · 36

S

salad · 102, 105-107
salt · 66-68
sausages · 32, 110
shrimp · 36
snails · 110
spaghetti · 74, 101, 124, 125
Spitini alla Siciliana · 41
steaks · 41
swordfish · 116

T

testicles, sheep · 33
tomatoes · 74, 105, 136
turmeric · 137

W

whipped cream · 49, 129
wild boar · 110
wine · 110
wine, red · 49, 113
wine, white · 13

Y

yogurt · 49

Z

zucchini · 124-125, 128

Resource List

Books:

The Inspector Montalbano series by Andrea Camilleri
The Leopard by Giuseppe Tomasi di Lampedusa
The Sicilian by Mario Puzo
A House in Sicily by Daphne Phelps
Sicily: A Literary Guide for Travellers by Andrew and Suzanne Edwards
The Stone Boudoir: In Search of the Hidden Villages of Sicily by Theresa Maggio.
The Dangerously Truthful Diary of a Sicilian Housewife by Veronica di Grigilo
Sicilian Food by Mary Taylor Simeti.
Bitter Almonds by Mary Taylor Simeti and Maria Grammatico
Palmento: A Sicilian Wine Odyssey by Roberto Camuto
Dorling Kindersley Eyewitness Travel Guide: Sicily (2015)
Lonely Planet Sicily (2013) available for Kindle
Top 10 Sicily (2014)
Frommer's Shortcut Sicily (2016)

Films:

L'Avventura (The Adventure) is a 1960 film directed by Michelangelo Antonioni.
Baarìa, directed by Giuseppe Tornatore and released in 2009.
Divorzio all'Italiana or *Divorce Italian Style* from 1961 and directed by Pietro Germi.

Nuovo Cinema Paradiso by director, Salvatore Di Vita, released in 1988.
Il Postino (1995) directed by Michael Radford.
Stromboli (1950) directed by Roberto Rossellini and starring Ingrid Bergman.
Il Gattopardo (The Leopard) released in 1963 starring Burt Lancaster and directed by Luchino Visconti.
Io Non Ho Paura (I Am Not Scared) from 2003 was directed by Gabriele Salvatores.
The Godfather series (1972, 1974, 1990) directed by Francis Ford Coppola starring (amongst others) Marlon Brando, Al Pacino, and Robert De Niro.
Diario di Una Siciliana Ribelle (The Sicilian Girl) (1997) directed by Marco Amenta.
Mafioso (1963) by director Alberto Lattuada
Lo Scambio (Hidden Identities) released in 2015 and directed by Salvo Cuccia.

Blogs and Websites:

www.mysicilianhome.wordpress.com
www.baroquesicily.com
www.lostinsicilia.com
siciliangodmother.com
unwillingexpat.wordpress.com
www.timesofsicily.com
www.bestofsicily.com
englishmaninitaly.org
www.beginningwithi.com/2006/08/30/share-your-experiences-with-telecom-italia
www.slowtrav.com/rebecca/20060105.htm
www.reidsitaly.com